GREENHOUSE GARDENING

Hamlyn Practical Gardening Guides

GREENHOUSE GARDENING

Sue Phillips

HAMLYN

Published in 1989 by
The Hamlyn Publishing Group Limited
a division of the Octopus Publishing Group
Michelin House
81 Fulham Road
London SW3 6RB

ISBN 0 600 564 827

Typeset by MS Filmsetting Limited, Frome, Somerset
Printed in Italy

CONTENTS

INTRODUCTION

Greenhouse gardening is gardening with a difference – you can grow a fascinating range of unusual and out of season vegetables, and even flowers for cutting. Furthermore, you can cultivate subtropical plants that don't flower or ripen properly outside in our climate.

The greenhouse is also a handy place to keep houseplants while they are recuperating, and you can have a lot of fun by raising all your own plants. It'll save you a fortune! If you get really hooked, it's easy to pursue an interest in a particular group of plants and end up with a specialist collection of perhaps cacti, fuchsias or geraniums.

The greenhouse gardening year starts in spring, with propagation playing a major part in your activities. There are seeds to sow, cuttings to take, and pricking out and potting up to follow on soon. It is also the time when greenhouse pot plants begin growing again after their winter rest, so you'll need to begin watering and feeding.

By early summer, edible crops like tomatoes and peppers can be planted, and everything will be growing away strongly. Keeping up with the watering will be your biggest job. This is when it is useful to shade the greenhouse and make use of semi-automatic watering.

In mid summer, keeping the greenhouse cool and humid is a problem. It helps to damp down the greenhouse with a cool spray of water over the floor, border soil and under the staging. Ideally do this early each morning and again at midday. Meanwhile plants are growing at their very fastest now, so keep well up to date with watering and feeding. It's also the most colourful time under glass if you grow pot plants.

Towards the end of summer, everything starts to slow down as the weather cools down. Gradually reduce watering and feeding as plants start to prepare for their winter rest. Take late cuttings of perennials like geraniums and fuchsias.

In autumn, tomatoes etc will be just about finished and need pulling out – any remaining fruit can be ripened indoors. This is the perfect time to clean the greenhouse and everything in it. By doing this, you'll cut down enormously on common winter greenhouse problems like fungal disease and slug damage. Watering should be reduced to a bare minimum when the weather is cold or foggy and dull.

In winter, there is very little to do in the way of chores, apart from removing dead leaves and making sure slugs, mice and other pests are kept at bay. Watering is rarely necessary as most plants are best kept very dry and feeding is not required.

Opposite: For the keen gardener, a greenhouse provides endless hours pleasure, greatly extending the range of plants which can be grown.

In summer, the greenhouse becomes a riot of colour with potted geraniums in shades of pink and red.

CHOOSING AND ERECTING
A GREENHOUSE

The first consideration is to decide what kind of greenhouse you want, which can be difficult given the huge number of different makes, shapes and sizes on the market. Your decision must be based on how much space you have and the range of plants you plan to grow.

LEAN-TO OR FREE-STANDING?
A free-standing greenhouse is the sort most people choose, but a lean-to can be much more practical if you only have a small garden. This is because it takes up space that might otherwise be left empty, perhaps next to a wall or over the back door. A lean-to can also be warmer than a free-standing greenhouse since one glass wall is replaced by brick, which retains the heat over a longer period. If the lean-to is built over a back door, you'll be surprised how much heat it traps escaping from the house. This not only helps save on your indoor central heating bill, but in a mild area can be sufficient to keep the lean-to free of frost in winter.

But while lean-to greenhouses are naturally warmer, a free-standing house receives more light. Provided it is correctly sited, there can be continuous sunlight, whereas a lean-to will be in the shade for at least part of the time, even if it has been built on the south side of the house. This makes a lean-to much more suitable for growing ornamental plants than for tomatoes or propagation, for which good light at all times is essential. In any case, being so close to the house ornamental plants in a lean-to can be admired.

WOODEN OR METAL FRAMES?
Cost is probably the most important consideration, with appearance and cheap maintenance being extra factors to consider. Aluminium greenhouses are undoubtedly cheaper to buy, but cedarwood, or other similar woods, do look very much nicer in the garden. On the practical side, metal greenhouses need no maintenance at all, whereas wooden

The glass-to-ground aluminium greenhouse is a popular choice, being suitable for growing plants in borders or pots on staging.

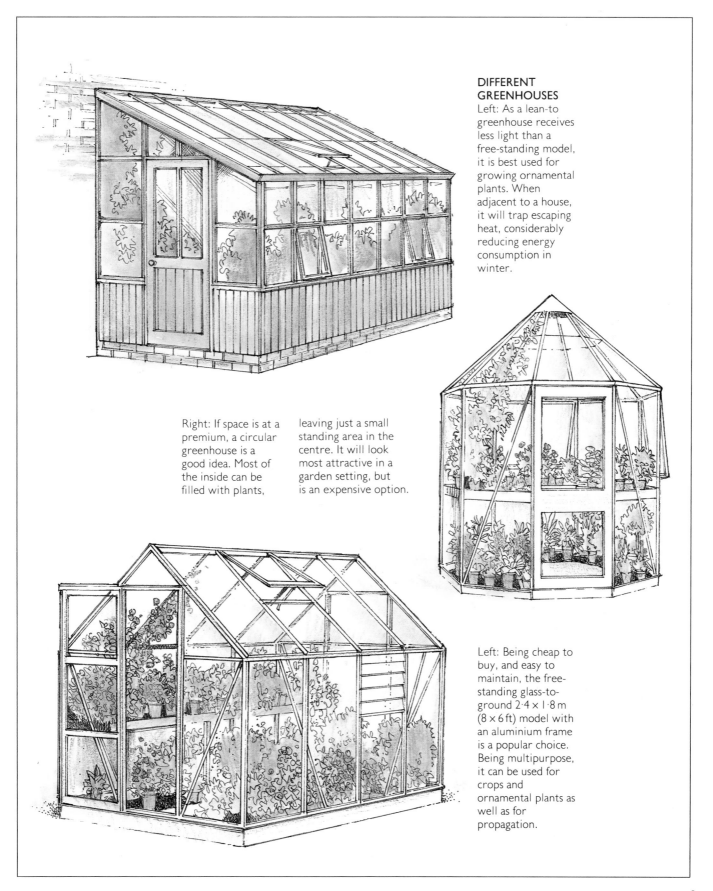

DIFFERENT GREENHOUSES
Left: As a lean-to greenhouse receives less light than a free-standing model, it is best used for growing ornamental plants. When adjacent to a house, it will trap escaping heat, considerably reducing energy consumption in winter.

Right: If space is at a premium, a circular greenhouse is a good idea. Most of the inside can be filled with plants, leaving just a small standing area in the centre. It will look most attractive in a garden setting, but is an expensive option.

Left: Being cheap to buy, and easy to maintain, the free-standing glass-to-ground 2·4 x 1·8 m (8 x 6 ft) model with an aluminium frame is a popular choice. Being multipurpose, it can be used for crops and ornamental plants as well as for propagation.

Careful use of space, with plants growing in borders, in pots on shelves and in hanging baskets, makes it possible to put together an impressive collection in the greenhouse.

structures will occasionally need painting with wood preservative to retain their colour and prevent rotting. Also note that wooden framed greenhouses are likely to retain heat slightly better than metal versions, which conduct heat away faster. On the other hand metal greenhouses will usually let in more light, because the glazing bars are much narrower than wooden ones.

RECTANGULAR OR ROUND?

Selecting the shape is a matter of comparing looks and space-saving against price. Most greenhouses are rectangular, but in very small gardens, or those where appearance is particularly important, a round greenhouse can be a much better idea. Since they are usually made of cedarwood, they look very attractive – like a small gazebo. What's more, there is no wasted space inside. The staging runs right the way round, leaving just a doorway and a small space in the middle where you stand. But attractive though they are, they have one disadvantage – the price!

WHAT SIZE?

There's an old saying about greenhouses – whichever size you buy, one year later you'll wish that you had bought one twice as big!

If money is no object, you can buy greenhouses as big as you like, right up to the size used by small commercial growers. But for many of us, the most sensible buy is the standard $2.4 \times 1.8\,m$ ($8 \times 6\,ft$) greenhouse, though in many cases that's been reduced to $2.1 \times 1.5\,m$ ($7 \times 5\,ft$). The reason – manufacturers can produce the most popular size more cheaply than any other! If you buy a standard size but later find you need more room, it is often possible to extend by building an identical greenhouse at one end. So if you think there is any chance this may happen, do check before siting your first greenhouse that there will be sufficient space for a second one. Also, make sure the design allows you to do this without keeping them separate, although this isn't a handicap. In fact, having two greenhouses can be an advantage, because you can heat one and use the other cold, or provide two completely different sets of growing conditions for different types of plants. Or, you can use one greenhouse for a general collection, and the other one for specialist use, such as growing exhibition chrysanthemums.

HEATED OR COLD?

Most people start with an unheated greenhouse, and add heating later if they need it. Although it is generally assumed a cold greenhouse is a bit limited in scope, it is surprising just how much you can grow without heat. In summer, for instance,

the greenhouse can be used for the same sort of crops as a heated greenhouse – tomatoes, melons, cucumbers, etc – plus a very good range of summer-flowering annual pot plants. The only difference is you can't start quite so early as in a heated greenhouse. You can also propagate winter-flowering pot plants, herbaceous garden flowers and shrub cuttings, since these don't need heat in the winter months.

Another use for a cold greenhouse is to

Below: Begonias, geraniums and fuchsias can all be grown in a cold greenhouse in summer.

Right: Grown in a cold greenhouse, spring bulbs such as *Narcissus triandrus* will bloom in winter.

grow a lot of interesting, out of season or exotic edibles – figs and grapes, early baby beetroot, new potatoes and finger carrots – as well as extra early strawberries, and you can grow lots of fascinating bulbs and alpines for winter flowers. It is even possible to grow frost-tender plants such as fuchsias, geraniums and tuberous begonias, provided you only keep them in the greenhouse between mid May and mid September, and then move them indoors to a warm windowsill for the winter.

The advantage of a heated greenhouse is that you can get everything off to an earlier start, and also have a later finish, while growing a much bigger range of plants. Tomatoes, for example, can be kept cropping almost until Christmas, while in an unheated greenhouse the cold would kill them off. You can also grow lots of winter-flowering pot plants and exotic greenhouse perennials, including collectables such as cacti and carnivorous plants.

The heat will also enable you to keep tender potted patio shrubs for the winter. You can begin your normal year's propagating earlier, and produce all your own bedding and tomato plants (which need an early start with plenty of heat). Of course, you no longer need to move all your geraniums, fuchsias and begonias indoors for the winter – you can just leave them in the greenhouse.

Finally, a heated greenhouse makes a very cosy winter retreat. It's a good place to take a cup of tea and the radio, while spending an hour or two pricking out seedlings. Or you could quite simply admire your plant collection! Winter-flowering pot plants should now be at their best, and early flowering bulbs and alpines will soon be flourishing.

PREPARING THE SITE AND ERECTING THE GREENHOUSE

THE RIGHT POSITION

In a very small garden, you probably won't have much choice where you site your greenhouse – it will have to go wherever there is room. But if you do have plenty of space, choose a site that gets plenty of sun all day long, well away from overhanging trees or nearby buildings that may shade it. Pick a well-sheltered spot where there is little risk of glass being broken by strong winds, and within hose-pipe distance of a tap for watering. If possible, also keep it close to the electricity supply in case you later decide to provide heat, light, and an electric propagator.

THE SITE

Regardless of whether you are building the greenhouse yourself or getting someone to do it for you, prepare the site well in advance. (Note: if you are paying a firm to construct the greenhouse, you'll usually find there is likely to be an extra charge for additional work such as levelling the ground and constructing the base for it.)

Preparing the site is not difficult, and merely involves making it level and uniformly firm so that it is ready for the foundations to be laid. However, many greenhouses, especially the metal kinds, now have pre-formed bases available as an optional extra. These are often made of metal and are easily assembled on the lines of a meccano set. The bases are lain on top of the prepared soil, with the greenhouse neatly being bolted into place.

If you don't buy the manufacturer's base, you will need to build a dwarf wall, about two or three bricks high for the greenhouse to be built on to. Needless to say, if you opt for this method it is vitally important to get your measurements exactly right.

Whether choosing a brick or metal base, it is essential to make sure that the base is perfectly level not only from side to side and front to back, but across the diagonals as well. Use a spirit level. If the base is at all skewed, you can be certain the greenhouse will be extremely difficult, if not completely impossible, to put up.

CONSTRUCTION

If you decide to build the greenhouse yourself, do read the manufacturer's instructions thoroughly before you start, and make quite sure you understand them. You should find they tell you everything you need to know.

It's always a good idea to begin by laying out all the parts. Use a felt tipped pen to label each piece so you can easily see what it is and where it goes according to the manufacturer's plan. Not only will this let you envisage how you must tackle the project, but it also enables you to check that all the pieces are there.

The structure is usually assembled flat on the ground, each side being constructed in turn before they are bolted to the base. The glazing bars in the roof are normally put in last. Allow a complete day for assembling the structure; don't start putting the glass in now, but leave this task for another day when you can complete the job all at once.

To glaze the greenhouse, you need a very still, dry day. Again, you can expect it to take virtually the whole day to finish. Don't worry about the shelving and staging while you are building the house. These items can easily be put up later, being constructed inside the greenhouse. It is essential you complete the glazing in one day. A half-glazed greenhouse could be damaged by overnight winds.

A greenhouse should be sited away from overhanging trees and tall buildings so it receives plenty of light.

Opposite: The standard aluminium frame free-standing greenhouse comes in a kit form that can be readily assembled.

RUNNING A GREENHOUSE

BASIC EQUIPMENT

There is no reason why you should not start using the greenhouse just as it is, without inserting any extra equipment. If you are planning to grow crops, such as tomatoes, in a bed within the greenhouse, you don't need any accessories. However, if you plan to do any propagating, or grow potted plants, then it is a good idea to put staging along one or both sides of the greenhouse.

Staging can be either slatted or solid, and made of aluminium or wood. Aluminium staging does not rust or rot, and is probably the most practical. Wooden staging may need attention in later life, though like wooden greenhouses it looks much more attractive. If you envisage using any kind of semi-automatic watering system, then choose solid staging. With slatted staging the plants tend to dry out faster as the air passes up through the gaps.

However, there is a third kind of staging available. This is very lightweight, often made of metal wire coated with plastic, and is secured at one end by hinges attached to the side of the greenhouse, while the front is supported on legs. The advantage of this form of staging is that it can easily be folded down, and stored flat against the side of the greenhouse taking up minimal space. This will be particularly useful if, for instance, you want to grow tomatoes in the border underneath.

Shelves are not essential, but some people find them a very useful way of making extra room for growing potted plants when all the staging has been filled. They can also look most effective when supporting trailing plants.

Another useful extra is a second roof ventilator. Most small greenhouses only have one vent fitted as standard, which really is not enough on a hot summer's day, unless you are able to prop the door open as well. Better still, put a louvered ventilator in a side wall. This will be particularly useful as it can be left open even on windy days without risk of damage, and, since it will be placed about halfway up the side of the greenhouse, it will create 'forced ventilation'. This term describes the process by which hot air rises, escaping through the open roof vent, while at the same time new cool air is drawn in through the louver in the side of the house. This gets the air moving through the greenhouse much faster than with a roof ventilator.

The other piece of equipment you'll find almost indispensable is an automatic ventilator opener. This saves you the bother of going down to the greenhouse every time the sun comes out, or whenever it turns dull, to open or close the ventilator. An auto-vent, as it is called, is very cheap and

Traditional tiered staging made from wooden slats will show off a collection of decorative potted plants in an attractively banked display, yet still make good use of the space available in the greenhouse.

Two storey aluminium staging is only suitable in a greenhouse which has glass down to ground level. Without this, the plants on the lower level – even shade-lovers – will receive insufficient light. The staging must be solid for watering if you plan to use capillary matting.

Temporary staging, secured to the side of the greenhouse by hinges, can be folded away when it is not required. Use it to raise bedding plants in spring, then put it away in summer, to free the ground below for cultivation.

easy to fit, and does not need to run off electricity, being powered by the sun's heat. The gadget is very simple, and consists of a sealed tube of paraffin wax, the contents of which expand and contract according to the temperature. When the paraffin wax expands, it acts like a piston and operates a 'plunger' device that is linked via a crank to the greenhouse ventilator, which is automatically raised or lowered. The typical auto-vent operates roof ventilators, but you can also get a specially designed version for opening the louvered ventilators.

THE BARE ESSENTIALS

Now that you've tackled the greenhouse, it's time to equip yourself for raising seeds and plants. First of all you need pots, seed trays, and composts.

Pots They come in a variety of sizes, such as 9 cm ($3\frac{1}{2}$ in) or 13 cm (5 in), the measurements denoting the distance across the top. The 9 cm ($3\frac{1}{2}$ in) pots are the most useful size for general purposes, but it's also handy to have a few larger ones – 13 cm (5 in) and 18 cm (7 in) for instance – plus a few half pots (the same distance across the top, but only half as deep).

Plastic pots are more commonly used, since they are cheaper to buy and much lighter in weight than the old clay pots. However, clay pots are useful for large, top-heavy plants, especially if they are likely to be stood outdoors for the summer – their weight makes them less likely to be blown over. If you are using clay pots in a glasshouse, you'll soon discover that modern greenhouse staging is not always sturdy enough to take the weight. The staging is designed mostly to support

plastic pots. So if you do use clay ones, it is best either to stand them on the floor or make your own staging. This can be done using a series of planks supported on bricks.

Seed trays They come in two sizes, full size and half size. The best sort to buy are made from polypropylene which can be washed in very hot water, and is almost impossible to break. Cheap plastic trays eventually become brittle and break, but since they are very cheap to replace, this barely matters.

The old wooden seed trays are rarely seen now, and though they look picturesque, are terribly difficult to clean and always seem to need repairing. If you don't want to buy seed trays, you can always adapt household objects instead. Old margarine tubs, vending cups, yoghurt pots, or strawberry punnets all make excellent alternatives.

Composts These are special mixtures for growing plants in, not the compost you make at the bottom of the garden! Proprietary composts are much better for plants growing in pots. Do not use garden soil – it is not as nutritious and will not produce such good results. Some gardeners mix their own composts, but this is not really a job for the beginner as it is very difficult to ensure the ingredients are evenly mixed.

Ready mixed composts come in two basic sorts, those made from peat (such as Levington), and those made from soil (John Innes). Some people prefer one kind

Trays are used for raising large numbers of plants from seed. Though trays this size will take up to 250 seedlings, try not to sow the seed too thickly.

and some another, so it's really a case of trying both and sticking to what you find works best for you. In practice, the main differences are in weight – soil is heavier than peat – and the fact that plants grown in peat composts need more feeding but less watering than those grown in the soil composts.

Both soil and peat-based composts come in several different types, according to what you intend growing. Seed composts are for sowing seeds or raising cuttings. Potting composts are suitable for most young plants from the time they are ready to be potted. You will also find ericaceous compost for growing lime-hating plants such as camellia and heathers; cactus compost for cacti and succulents; and occasionally special composts for growing orchids, or other plants with particular needs.

If you are a beginner, one bag of seed, and one of potting compost is all you need to get started. Or if you want to buy just one bag, choose a universal compost (sometimes called sowing and potting compost) which can be used for both jobs. Either way, always use bought composts straight from the bag – there is no need to mix them with anything – and keep the top rolled firmly down and secured after use so no weed seeds, or diseases can get inside.

PROPAGATING

This is one of the most exciting parts of greenhouse gardening. If you want to take up plant propagation seriously, then an efficient, electrically heated and thermostatically controlled propagator will enable you to have a high success rate all the year round. But if you only want to do a little propagating, perhaps in spring or summer when cuttings and seeds are easiest to grow, you can get by with nothing more than a few seed trays. Buy or make transparent plastic seed tray covers, which will create a beneficial humid atmosphere when water is sprayed within.

PROPAGATING FROM SEED

This is normally a spring job, though there are some plants (such as annual winter-flowering pot plants, and garden perennials and biennials) that are sown in mid summer. Some plants, such as shrubs and hardy annuals for early flowering the next spring, may be sown in early autumn.

The key to successful seed raising is cleanliness. Everything you use – pots, trays, plastic covers and the propagator itself – must be perfectly clean. You must

Space sow large seeds, setting them approximately 2·5 cm (1 in) apart in rows on the surface of the seed compost. Press them gently into the compost to cover.

Wax begonias (*Begonia semperflorens*) are grown as half-hardy annuals. They can be raised from seed in the greenhouse in February and March and then planted out as soon as danger of frost is over in flowerbeds, windowboxes, hanging baskets and tubs.

therefore begin by washing out everything you intend to use in warm water and washing-up liquid, followed by a rinse in a solution of garden disinfectant and then a good final rinse in some clean water. You must also use fresh seed sowing compost. (Don't buy more at one time than you can use within a few weeks, and keep the top of the bag rolled down after it has been opened to prevent disease organisms getting into it.)

To sow seed, fill a tray or small pot loosely with compost, level it across the top, and then firm it very gently down with a flattener – a small piece of wood you have cut to fit the inside of the pot or tray. Sow small seeds by scattering them evenly over the surface of the compost. Cover them to their own depth with a fine sprinkling of compost. Very tiny seeds are best not covered at all, but left on the surface of the compost. Large seeds, such as sweet peas, are best 'space sown' – laid out about 2·5 cm (1 in) apart in rows all over the surface of the compost, and then gently pressed in until they are just covered (this makes them easier to separate when they come up).

Water the seeds by standing the seed container in several centimetres of water until the compost turns a dark colour –

this indicates that the water has soaked right through to the top. Then place the pot or tray inside the propagator or under a plastic cover. If you don't have either, stand the container of seeds inside a large plastic bag, for humidity, keeping the bag well away from the soil using a twig or stick. Then place the container in a well-shaded spot but not in the dark, because many seeds need light to germinate.

Seeds sown in late spring will not need extra heat, but if you sow early in the season a heated propagator is advisable, as is a heated greenhouse to grow the seedlings on. The temperature should be set according to that recommended on the seed packet, 16°–21°C (60°–70°F) being normal. Take a look at the seeds occasionally and water as often as is necessary to keep the compost just moist.

Remove the containers from their plastic bags when the first shoots begin to emerge. However, the seeds being raised in a propagator or under cover can stay put for a while, but do open the ventilator slots in the tops to provide them with fresh air, or they may start 'damping off' (being attacked by a fungal disease, marked by wilting and rotting). When the seedlings have grown their first pair of leaves (seed leaves), they are ready for 'pricking out',

though if they are well spaced apart you can leave them in their seed trays a bit longer before moving them.

To prick out seedlings, prepare a tray or pot of fresh seed compost in the same way as described for seed sowing. Lift each seedling out by a leaf, after loosening the roots with a pointed stick or dibber. (Don't handle seedlings by their stems – if you bruise them they can die.) Now make a hole with your pointed stick, big enough to take the roots, and plant the seedling up to its neck, with the seed leaves just resting above the compost level. This is important, or you will get tall leggy seedlings that easily die. Space the seedlings about 2·5–5 cm (1–2 in) apart, depending on their size, and when you have filled the tray or pot, water the seedlings in with a fine rose on the end of a watering can spout, or by standing the tray in several centimetres of water. Keep the newly pricked out seedlings well shaded for a few weeks while they acclimatize.

Seedlings that were germinated in a propagator should ideally be returned to the propagator for a week or so after pricking out. Over this period you should gradually lower the temperature and increase the ventilation to get the seedlings acclimatized to life in the open.

GREENHOUSE GARDENING

PROPAGATING FROM CUTTINGS

Many plants can be propagated from cuttings taken at any time between early spring and late summer. Late summer is a good time to strike cuttings of plants such as geraniums and fuchsias because they will root before winter, and can be left in their trays or small pots ready for final potting the following spring.

Cuttings rooted the previous autumn will start flowering much earlier than spring-struck cuttings. However, some garden plants – such as chrysanthemum, dahlia, delphinium, etc – are usually grown from cuttings taken very early in the spring. This is deliberately done to allow the young plants enough time to develop adequately and flower during the season. Any plants with corms, such as tuberous begonias, are also best propagated from cuttings in spring. This gives them enough time to grow a new corm, which is essential if they are going to survive the winter. There are several different types of cuttings.

Tip cuttings They are the commonest means of taking a cutting, and are obtained from any plant that has normal stems such as geraniums, fuchsias, etc.

To take tip cuttings, prepare and fill pots or seed trays as when sowing seeds. Use a sharp knife or secateurs to snip off 7·5–10 cm (3–4 in) from the ends of young shoots. Then trim the cutting by making a clean cut with a very sharp knife just

Above: Geranium cuttings usually take four to six weeks to root. When they start producing new leaves at the top, check to see if they have rooted and pot on.

Left: Ivy-leaved geraniums can be enjoyed year after year, if you take cuttings from them in late summer.

below the lowest leaf joint. Next, remove the leaves from the bottom half of the cutting, and any flowers or buds. Then dip the cut end of the shoot into rooting powder. Push the cutting into the compost to about half its length, spacing each one about 5 cm (2 in) apart. (It is usual to put four or five cuttings into a 9 cm [$3\frac{1}{2}$ in] pot; a tray is only used if you have two dozen or so cuttings.) Water the cuttings in by either standing them in water, as for seed, or by using a fine rose on a watering can.

If you take cuttings before the middle of May, it helps them to root if you place the pot in a plastic bag, under a cover, or in a heated propagator. But if you take them later in the spring, or in summer, when they are easier to root, most cuttings will grow perfectly well in a shady spot provided they are kept just moist and humid. Hairy leaved cuttings should never be put in a polythene bag to root as too much humidity tends to make them rot.

Regularly look at your cuttings. Water them whenever they need it, pick off any dead leaves, and check to see if they have rooted. Stem cuttings normally take from four to six weeks to root. You can tell when they are ready for potting on as the cutting starts to grow and produce new leaves from the top. You may also see roots growing out through the holes in the bottom of the pots or trays, a sure sign that they need a larger pot.

Leaf cuttings Plants that do not have shoots, where the leaves grow from a central rosette or rootstock, as with tuberous begonias and streptocarpus, are grown from leaf cuttings. This method requires a whole leaf, complete with its stalk. (It must be a fairly young leaf from near the centre of a plant but which has entirely opened out.) It can be treated just like a tip cutting, with its stalk being pushed into a pot of compost. Or, if you want lots of cuttings, you can slice up the leaf into squares about the same size as a postage stamp, and push them edgeways into a tray of compost, leaving half of each cutting sticking out.

Cuttings made from a whole leaf root easily, but the cut-up squares must be treated with care – if they dry out they will shrivel up and fail to root. It is therefore best to lay a sheet of cling-film polythene loosely over them after watering. This can

be left on for four to five weeks. Leaf cuttings should be left in their trays until you can see new shoots growing up from the compost, which indicates that they have rooted and begun to make new plants. This is the time to pot them. Keep newly potted cuttings well-shaded for a few weeks, while they acclimatize.

PROPAGATING BY DIVISION
Plants that naturally form clumps instead of growing from one main stem can be propagated by division. This will immediately provide you with a supply of new plants. There's no waiting while roots grow, and little likelihood of failure. Suitable plants for dividing include aspidistra, and asparagus and maidenhair ferns.

Some plants such as mother-in-law's tongue don't clump, but produce offsets instead; these are like little plants that grow a short distance away from the parent. To take an offset split up a large potful of plants to make several new ones. The best time to split up plants in this way is in the spring when they start growing, or in autumn when they stop.

Knock the plant carefully out of its pot, and carefully prise the ball of roots apart with your fingers. Divide it into two or three pieces, each of which contains a roughly equal portion of plant. Try to avoid breaking off any roots, or removing more compost from the root ball than you have to. If the roots are too solidly packed for you to divide with your hands, use a long knife instead and cut through

the root ball to separate each new clump. Trim off the damaged bits of root afterwards, and dust the cut ends with rooting powder. Then pot up each section of plant individually. Water, and keep them shaded for a week or so while they get established.

Plants cut apart with a knife should be kept slightly drier to start with, to prevent damaged roots from rotting.

POTTING AND REPOTTING
When cuttings have rooted, and seedlings which previously have been pricked out have filled their tray, they are ready for potting. Since the young plants will have a reasonably good root system, they can be grown in potting compost from now on. If using John Innes compost, choose No. 1 which is the weakest and most suitable mix for potting young plants. Otherwise, use a peat-based potting compost or a multi-purpose seed and potting compost.

For the first potting, 9 cm ($3\frac{1}{2}$ in) pots are normally the best size to use. You should begin with a pot only a little larger than the young plant's root system, and repot into a larger size each time the pot fills with root, moving the plant to a pot one size bigger each time. Plants don't grow so well if you put them in too big a pot to start with.

To pot up a young plant, remove it carefully from its previous tray or pot, disturbing the root ball as little as possible. Place just a little fresh compost in

REPOTTING
1. Repot a plant when its roots have filled the pot. Remove it carefully, trying not to disturb the root ball.
2. Place a little fresh compost in a new, larger pot, and then stand the plant in it. Fill in around the roots with more compost.
3. Fill almost to the top of the pot with compost, and then firm down well.

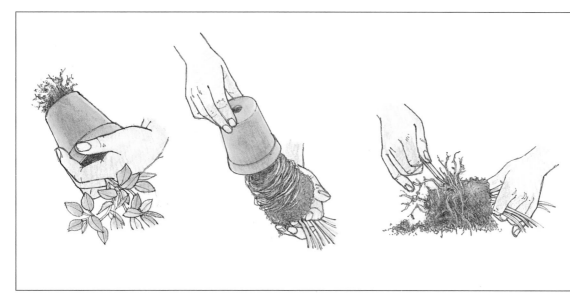

POT BOUND
1. A plant is pot bound when its roots start growing out of the drainage hole.
2. When you knock it out of its pot, you will see that the roots coil around the outside of the root ball.
3. Tease a few of the large roots out from the tangle, so that when you repot they can start growing out in the new compost.

the bottom of the new pot, and stand the plant in it. Hold it loosely in place, well centred, while you fill in around the roots with more compost. Fill almost to the top of the pot, and then firm the compost very lightly down with your fingers. Check the plant is still at the same depth it was originally growing, and water it well. Always grow newly potted plants in slightly shaded conditions for a few weeks before moving them into full sun. This will help them get their new roots properly established.

It's impossible to give one absolute period after which plants will require a larger pot and more space for their root system, because they grow at different rates. So the best way to check if this is necessary is by looking underneath the pot. If roots are growing out through the drainage holes, it is time to repot. Choose a pot one size larger than the old one and repeat the same process as before. Avoid breaking up the ball of roots, unless the plant is badly pot bound, with the roots tightly coiled around the edge of the old pot forming a solid mass which is difficult to tease apart. In this case, it is a good idea to loosen gently a few of the thick coiled roots from the bottom of the root ball, helping them start spreading out into the fresh compost in the new pot.

Annual plants will probably never need

If a greenhouse is built on good soil, dig the border for growing tomatoes, chrysanthemums and other tall plants.

potting into anything larger than a 13 cm (5 in) pot or half pot. But long-lived greenhouse plants, such as lemon trees, aspidistra, figs or grape vines, grown in pots will probably end up in very large containers indeed – perhaps 30–38 cm (12–15 in). By the time they reach pots this size you clearly cannot keep transferring plants into a larger pot each time they need it. The solution is to top dress the pots once a year, in the spring, just as new growth begins. Scrape away the top layer of old soil and replace it with new potting compost. If you use John Innes compost, then No. 3 is ideal for potting large plants or top dressing them. Otherwise you can just as easily use your usual potting or multi-purpose compost.

PLANTING INTO THE BORDER

Not all of the plants you raise in the greenhouse will be grown in pots throughout their lives. Some, such as tomato, pepper, lettuce and cucumber plants, will be planted out in the greenhouse border.

In the early stages these plants are grown in the same way as pot plants, with individual seedlings being pricked out into trays or small pots. But instead of potting them on as you would pot plants, they are planted out into the border. With edible crops particularly, it is very important to plant them out as soon as the pot or tray they are growing in is filled with roots. You can tell when this is happening just by looking at the bottom of the pots – in the case of plastic containers and trays you can see the roots just starting to grow out of the holes in the bottom, and if you use peat pots, you'll see roots starting to appear through the sides.

Don't let the plants get pot bound, or they will suffer a bad check in growth and take a long time to recover – which means your crop will be late starting. If by chance plants do become pot bound, give them a good soaking in diluted liquid feed, at its normal strength, before planting, and tease out the largest roots from the coiled mass when you plant. Make sure the ground is well prepared before planting, so it has a light consistency.

To plant, make a hole slightly bigger than the root ball of each plant, knock the plants gently out of their pots or trays (if grown in peat pots, plant the pot too) and

sit the root ball in place. Do not damage the root ball. Fill in around it with soil, leaving it at the same depth it was growing in its pot. Then water it well.

STOPPING, PRUNING, TRAINING AND TIDYING

Many greenhouse pot plants, such as geraniums and fuchsias, tend to become tall and leggy. If left to their own devices they can look rather flimsy and insubstantial, instead of being bushy shaped, more interesting, and decked with greater numbers of flowers.

Trained as standards, fuchsias make a good display in a greenhouse for decorative plants.

To encourage plants to become bushy, it is usual to stop them once or twice soon after they are potted. This means pinching out the growing point of the plant between your thumb and forefinger, just above a leaf. You can do this either when you pot the plant up, or wait until it has been growing for one to two weeks. Soon after, three or four new shoots will sprout from lower down on the stem.

If you want to grow an especially bushy

STANDARD FUCHSIAS

1. To grow a standard fuchsia, pot up an upright plant, and tie it, at intervals, to a 90 cm (3 ft) long split cane, to encourage it to remain straight.

2. Pinch out the side shoots as they appear, leaving only the main stem intact. Continue to tie the stem to the cane as it grows.

3. When the main stem reaches 15 cm (6 in) above the cane, pinch out the growing tip. Leave the side shoots to form the standard's head.

4. Allow the side shoots to grow 5 cm (2 in) long, then pinch out their growing tips. Repeat with new side shoots until a good ball-shaped head has formed.

the top. Fuchsias are often grown this way, though you can also train geraniums and many other perennial plants – even grape vines – as standards.

To grow your own standard plant, select a strong cutting with a straight stem and root it. When you pot it, do not pinch out the growing point. Instead, place a 90 cm (3 ft) cane in the pot by its side (you can grow a taller standard if you like, simply by using a taller cane) and, as the stem grows, tie it loosely to the cane with raffia or string. Pinch out any side shoots that grow, leaving only the single main stem. When it reaches the top of the cane, allow the shoot to produce an extra 15 cm (6 in) of growth and then pinch out the top. This time, do not remove the side shoots that grow. They will form the head of your standard.

When these shoots are 5 cm (2 in) long, pinch out the tips of their growing points. And when they produce side shoots once again pinch out the growing points after 5 cm (2 in). Keep doing this until you have an attractive, densely packed, rounded head. Don't expect results immediately though – it will probably take two years to grow a good specimen – and remember, always keep the head of the standard securely tied to the supporting cane, or it may be broken off.

As a change from normal standards, you can can also train plants such as box or bay into pyramids or fancy topiary shapes. These make fascinating specimens for patios or tubs outside a front door, though if growing dubiously hardy specimens, it is advisable to keep them in the greenhouse for winter.

In addition to stopping, pruning and training, which are only done occasionally, most ornamental greenhouse plants also need a little regular tidying to keep them looking their best. So check them over frequently and remove any dead leaves and flowers, nipping dead stems right back to where they join a healthy stem. This not only keeps plants looking tidy, but encourages them to produce new flowers, and helps prevent the occurrences of plant diseases.

plant that you intend potting on into a bigger pot at a later stage, you could even stop the plant a second time, a few weeks later. This time you should pinch out the growing tips of each of the new shoots when they are 5–7.5 cm (2–3 in) long. Older plants that have lost their shape, or are getting too big, can be pruned back to improve their appearance and keep them to a manageable size. This is normally only necessary for perennial plants, such as the eucalyptus or other greenhouse shrubs, which you will be keeping for several years.

Pruning is a useful way of rejuvenating old geraniums and fuchsias when you

want to keep them instead of propagating new ones. The best time to prune is in the autumn, when plants have finished their growth, or in early spring just as growth starts. But if necessary it can be done during the growing season. Plants can either be cut back hard, to within several centimetres of the top of the pot, or pruned lightly to remove straggly branches, so reshaping the plant. Either way, use sharp secateurs and cut just above a leaf joint, or just above the junction of a new shoot with an old stem.

Some kinds of plants are occasionally trained as standards – tall stems with a ball-shaped head of flowers and foliage at

WATERING

Watering will probably take up more of your time in the greenhouse than any other task. But watering isn't as easy as it sounds. Unfortunately, there are no hard and fast rules – you can't say you should water once a day or once a week – what matters is that you water when the plants need it, and the only way to check if they do is by regularly examining them.

With plants growing in the greenhouse border, it's easy to tell when they need watering because the soil surface looks and feels dry. Provided the soil is given an occasional thorough soaking, plants growing there can last quite a long time between waterings without ill effect, for their roots have access to a great deal of mois-

ture. In summer, the border may only need damping over daily, with a thorough soaking once a week. In winter, even if you are growing vegetable or salad crops, the border will hardly need watering at all provided it was soaked well before the crops were planted.

Pots, on the other hand – especially small ones – dry out very quickly in summer, when you will probably need to water them at least once a day, particularly during a hot spell. In winter, they won't need watering nearly so often – once a week at the most. If in doubt about when to water, it is best to check by testing the

compost with your finger or a special watering meter. Push the tip of your finger, or the point of the water meter, about 2·5 cm (1 in) into the pot. The meter will indicate how wet or dry the compost is; but with the finger method you have to judge for yourself whether the compost is bone dry, just right or too wet, and decide whether to water or not.

AUTOMATIC HELP
If you are out at work during the day, you may find it is difficult to find enough time to water the greenhouse regularly. However, the problem is solved by using one of the automatic watering devices now on the market. They usually work by having a tank or large plastic bag full of water hanging from the roof of the greenhouse, from which plastic tubes slowly leak water directly into pots or border soil, which are kept permanently just moist. All you have to do is top up the tank.

Another system uses special water matting (known as capillary matting) which is laid across the staging, beneath the pot plants. The tubes from the overhead tanks or bag of water then leak into the matting, which is kept permanently moist, allowing the plants standing on it to draw up as much water as they require. The advantage of this system is that it is much cheaper than those which require a tube to be inserted into each pot.

If you are good at DIY, you can easily make your own automatic watering system, using sheets of capillary matting that you can buy individually. The very simplest home-made scheme involves nothing more than standing plants on staging which has been covered with capillary matting, and wetting the matting thoroughly with a hose pipe each morning. You can also use strips of the matting to water large pots standing on the floor. Fill a bucket with water, and drape strips of the matting so that one end hangs in the bucket, with the other being tucked into the compost of a nearby pot. Provided you don't use one bucket of water to supply too many plants, you should find this is adequate for a day, or possibly even a weekend.

Small pot plants such as cyclamen should be watered only when the compost feels dry in winter.

For longer periods of time, perhaps while you are on a two-week holiday, it is best to take an alternative approach. Remove the pot plants from the greenhouse and plunge them up to their rims in soil in a damp shady part of the garden. Give them a good soak just before you go away, and they should still be fine when you get back.

During the colder season (mid September to mid March or early April), the golden rule for watering is, 'If in doubt, don't'. This is because when the weather is dull, plants do not grow so fast, and they don't need nearly so much water. If you have been using semi-automatic watering in summer, stop and return to hand watering instead. Plants will no longer require a continuous supply of water, only a feed once (or even less) per week.

Some plants become dormant during the winter months and need no water whatsoever, the corms of tuberous begonias being a good example. Others, like geraniums and fuchsias, are semi-dormant and can safely be left dry for long periods of time with only very occasional and modest watering.

FEEDING

In addition to watering, you will also need to feed greenhouse plants fairly frequently during the growing season. Although seed and potting composts contain plant food, it only lasts a short time. Once it has been used up, it has to be replaced by regular feeding of some kind.

The best products to use, for both potted plants and those in the border, are either liquid or soluble feeds, or the new slow-release feeds (which mostly come as sticks or granules).

Liquid and soluble feeds are mixed with water and applied with a watering can. They should be used regularly throughout the growing season. Slow-release feeds are more convenient if you don't have time for regular feeding. They are applied only occasionally, about every three months. To apply this sort of slow-release feed, you just scatter it over the compost or press it in, and it dissolves bit by bit, releasing a little plant food every time you water the pots or it rains.

The plant foods to avoid using in pots are solid fertilizers which are for outdoors. They are risky to use where roots are in a restricted space as the strong chemical concentration can easily scorch or kill the roots and harm the plant.

There are countless brands of plant food available. Any good general-purpose feed is fine for most greenhouse plants. But if you grow tomatoes, they will require a feed high in potash to encourage heavy fruiting, so in this instance use special liquid tomato feed.

Another method of feeding plants involves a foliar treatment. Instead of watering the feed into the soil, you spray it on to the leaves. Foliar feeding is therefore a very useful way of feeding plants that don't have much root, such as young seedlings or cuttings, or plants whose roots have been damaged perhaps by rotting or insect attack. It is also a good way of giving plants a quick boost, in spring, or when they are recovering from ill-health. You can apply a foliar feed and root feed at the same time to plants that are growing fast.

Special foliar feed products are available, though many normal liquid or soluble feeds can also be used as foliar feeds, provided they are diluted more than usual. When using foliar feeds, follow the normal precautions for spraying – take care not to use a sprayer that has previously been used for weedkiller, and avoid spraying on hot days or when the sun is on the plants.

Whichever method of feeding you choose, the golden rule is always follow the manufacturer's instructions as to the dilution rate and the frequency of feeding. As a rough guide, plants will need feeding regularly when they are growing fast in summer, and hardly at all, if ever, in winter. The need for feeding varies, too, according to a plant's stage of growth. Seedlings or cuttings are unlikely to need feeding until after they have been potted – the seed compost provides enough feed until this time.

Plants that have just been potted or repotted into new compost will not need feeding until they too have used up the available nutrition. This will take from six to eight weeks in a peat compost, and a few weeks longer in a soil-based compost. Bear in mind that plants grown in soil-based composts will need feeding less often than those which are grown in peat-based composts.

Right: The individual pot system, in which water passes from a header tank down a main tube and then into smaller tubes which lead to specific pots, is generally used for watering large pot plants – using this system for an extensive selection of small pot plants would involve too many tubes.

AUTOMATIC WATERING
Left: Water from a header tank, secured to the side of the greenhouse, passes slowly but continuously through layflat tubing which lies across the capillary matting. This layflat tubing is stitched along one side, allowing water to seep out on to the matting.

A traditional sprayer is ideal for applying a foliar feed to the leaves of plants, though you should be careful not to use equipment which has previously held weedkillers. When applying liquid or soluble feeds to the plant compost, use an ordinary watering can.

If all this sounds a bit vague, that's because plants are individuals growing at different rates, according to their size, health, age, the weather, and many other factors. But with practice, you'll find you can soon start to tell when a plant needs more feeding – its rate of growth will slow down, its foliage will tend to be yellowish green instead of deep green, and there may be fewer flowers or new buds produced. Shorter flower stems are another sign of food shortage.

VENTILATION

Whenever the sun comes out, the temperature inside a greenhouse rises sharply. But while plants like warmth, too much heat will make them dry out fast and wilt, and can even kill them. Ventilation is therefore essential for keeping the temperature down to a level at which plants will thrive. Ideally you should keep the greenhouse below 27°C (80°F), though provided plants are well watered they should be able to survive slightly higher temperatures for short spells.

Ventilation is also vital for letting fresh air into the greenhouse. Plants require carbon dioxide, as well as water, nutrients and sunlight, and if any one of these ingredients is in short supply, they won't grow properly. So constant ventilation is essential for topping up the carbon dioxide in the greenhouse, replacing that used by the plants.

Most greenhouses come equipped with a single ventilator in the roof. This is usually adequate, provided you are around during the day to open and close the door of the house for extra ventilation. If not, it is a good idea to put in an extra ventilator, either in the roof or in the side of the house, as described under Basic Equipment (see page 14).

Another useful extra is an automatic ventilator opener (see pages 14 to 15). This varies the amount of ventilation according to the temperature. An auto-vent is essential if you are away from home during the day, but even if you are about you will still find one very useful. Don't worry if you discover the ventilator open in the evening or in winter – provided it has been correctly installed it will only open when the temperature inside the greenhouse needs it

open – and it's surprising how the heat can build up. If you don't have automatic openers, it is a good idea to open the vents in the winter for an hour or two in the middle of the day, if the weather is fine, just to let in some fresh air. Don't forget to close them again before night fall.

SHADING

During the height of summer even good ventilation is not sufficient to keep the temperature down. Not only will plants suffer badly from the heat; many delicate plants, including young seedlings and shade-loving varieties, can be scorched and killed by exposure to the strong, direct sunlight.

To prevent both problems you must shade the greenhouse. Most people do it by painting the outside of the glass with a special greenhouse shading liquid. It resembles a weak white emulsion paint, which washes off easily at the end of the summer, allowing maximum light into the greenhouse for the rest of the year. For more temporary shading, old net curtains or sheets can be draped over a framework of canes or strings inside the greenhouse. This is a very useful way of shading young seedlings at the beginning of the season, when you may not want to paint the more long-lasting shading over the glass panes.

HEATING

By the time you have too many plants to bring indoors for the winter, you'll have to start thinking about heating the greenhouse. To be certain of keeping tender plants, such as geraniums, fuchsias, etc, safely through the winter, you will need to heat the greenhouse from the first frost in autumn until there is no more risk of serious frost the following spring. In practice, this means from around mid to late September, until late April or mid May, depending on where you live.

CUTTING YOUR COSTS

Heating can, of course, be expensive. To cut costs, try to keep the heat down as low as possible, without putting the plants at risk. Most commonly grown greenhouse plants can be kept through the winter at a temperature of 3·5°–4·5°C (38°–40°F), which is just enough to prevent a frost.

If you are only providing such background heat, it is essential to keep the plants as dry as possible, otherwise there is a big risk of them rotting or going mouldy. It is also advisable to spray them every few weeks (on fine days) with a fungicide as a precaution. If you want to keep more exotic plants, you will need to provide a little extra heat, from 7·5–10°C (45°–50°F). But provided there are only a few plants requiring this much warmth there is no need to heat the whole greenhouse to 10°C (50°F). You could either section off part of the greenhouse with polythene to keep it warmer, or move the exotic plants indoors to spend the winter on a windowsill.

TYPES OF HEATER

There are three basic kinds of heater – paraffin, gas or electric.

Paraffin heaters were popular a few years ago, being cheap to buy and run. But sadly this is no longer true, for the price of paraffin has since risen considerably. Another disadvantage is that as paraffin

heaters do not have thermostatic controls, you will always have to light them in the evening, fill them, and turn them off in the morning, which may not be convenient. Nor can you adjust the temperature – such heaters are either on or off. If you go to work on a cold winter's morning you may have to leave the heater running, despite the fact that the weather can greatly improve later in the day.

Gas heaters are much more convenient. They are available with thermostatic controls and will run for some time before you need to fit a new gas cylinder. Some gas heaters will run off the mains, but they are even more expensive to purchase than those needing gas cylinders. The big advantage of both paraffin and gas heaters is

that they can be used in a greenhouse which does not have electricity.

Electricity If available, it is the most reliable form of heating and the most economical. By using an accurate thermostat, the heat is only on when you need it, and cuts out the minute the required temperature is reached, so you don't waste any fuel. As electric heaters can be left to switch themselves on and off, you can go away for a few days without needing to worry. Another advantage is that they give out dry heat which discourages moisture-loving fungal diseases in winter. The only possible problem can be a power cut. So if you have a valuable plant collection, it pays to keep a small paraffin heater as well, as a stand by.

CLEANING

Once a year it is a good idea to give the greenhouse a thorough clean out. The best time for this may not in fact be the spring, since this can be a very busy time of year. Autumn is usually more convenient for most gardeners.

Choose a fine day, when the weather is warm and sunny, and empty the greenhouse entirely. Take out all the plants, together with any pots, canes, etc, that have accumulated under the staging, and pull up any weeds from the path and border. Then scrub down the inside of the glass, frame, staging, shelves, paving slabs or concrete floor, and anything else that is left permanently in place, with warm water and detergent, and a soft brush. Scrape off any moss or algae grow-ing on the glass, paying special attention to the cracks where adjacent glass panes overlap.

Next, wash everything inside the house, including the glass, with clean water and garden disinfectant, and drench the borders thoroughly with more of the same solution. Finally, rinse everything down with a strong jet of water from the hose, and leave the door and ventilators open so that the house can dry out before returning all the plants.

In the meantime, take this opportunity to tidy up plants that will be going back inside, removing all the dead leaves or flower heads, and cleaning up any dirty pots. Empty pots are best stored away from the greenhouse in winter as they often provide homes for mice, woodlice, etc, but if they have to be stored under the staging wash them well with a solution of greenhouse disinfectant before putting them back. If you clean the greenhouse in autumn, wash off any remaining shading from the outside of the glass at the same time, to improve winter light.

Your last task is to prepare the borders for planting. Fork them over, and dig in plenty of peat, well-rotted manure or garden compost to improve the soil. Rake the soil level, and remove any large stones, dead leaves and other debris. There is no need to add fertilizer before planting or sowing in the autumn. But before planting or sowing spring crops, sprinkle 96–128 g (3–4 oz) of solid fertilizer to every $\frac{1}{2}$ sq m (1 sq yd) of border, and rake it in lightly .

Opposite: Paraffin heaters are one way of keeping a greenhouse frost-free in winter.

Right: Clean the greenhouse once a year. Scrub all the glass panes with clean water and a garden disinfectant, and then rinse well with a strong jet of water.

PLANTS FOR THE COLD GREENHOUSE

ORNAMENTAL PLANTS

ALPINES

Alpines and other small rock plants make very attractive pot plants to grow in an unheated greenhouse in winter. The best kind to choose are those that flower in early spring and those with interestingly shaped forms or colours. Many such species grow better under glass than out in the garden, as they are protected from damp, which does them more harm than the cold.

Interesting kinds Look for pasque flowers, saxifrages (some of which are grown for early flowers, and some for their fascinating silvery rosette-like form); sempervivums (available as the familiar cobwebbed houseleek [*Sempervivum arachnoideum*], and varieties with red or red-tipped leaves); and many kinds of small, winter and early spring flowering

The rich blue and yellow flowers of *Iris reticulata* 'Harmony' make a stunning display in late winter. Their delicate scent is an added attraction.

Opposite: Pasque flowers (*Anemone pulsatilla*), which come in white or crimson forms as well as the stunning shade of purple seen here, bloom in spring. Try to avoid repotting these alpines as they resent root disturbance.

Alpine plants in the greenhouse are best grown on solid staging covered with shingle. This ensures free drainage of moisture from the pots – an essential requirement for these plants.

28

Winter display Although annuals are normally planted in May to flower over the rest of the summer, you can also grow some types under glass in winter for an early show of flowers in the greenhouse in spring. You must choose hardy annuals – suitable kinds include dwarf pot marigolds (*Calendula*), nasturtium, clarkia, and Beauty of Nice stocks. They can be sown under cold glass in late summer or autumn, and potted when big enough to handle. They will flower in the greenhouse early the following spring. Throw the old plants away when they have finished flowering or, if you want room for other plants before then, put the annuals out in the garden.

BULBS
Spring-flowering bulbs are useful for providing early spring colour in a cold greenhouse, where they will flower several weeks earlier than out of doors. The most successful kinds for growing in pots are small species, and dwarf growing varieties such as *Narcissus triandrus albus*, 'February Gold', 'Jenny', and 'Tête à Tête' for example.

bulbs such as hardy cyclamen, *Iris reticulata*, and miniature narcissi, including *N. bulbocodium* and *N. cyclamineus*.

Cultivation Grow alpines in a gritty compost, similar to that used for cacti. Or make your own alpine compost by mixing half and half John Innes potting compost No. 1 and horticultural grit. Stand the plants outside in the garden over summer, and avoid overwatering at all times. Most kinds need a sunny position, but a few, such as alpine primulas, prefer some shade. Protect plants from slugs and mice, especially in the winter months.

ANNUAL BEDDING PLANTS
Many annual bedding plants that are normally planted outside in the garden, make very pretty pot plants for growing under glass in summer. The advantage of growing them this way is that if you live in a cold or windy area the plants will grow and flower much better under cover than out in the garden. This is particularly true of varieties, such as petunias, whose blooms can get badly battered by adverse weather conditions.

Making a choice Select dwarf varieties for use as pot plants because of their compact growth, though trailing and

climbing annuals can be good too. Try petunias, black-eyed Susan (*Thunbergia*), busy Lizzie (*Impatiens*), salvia, ageratum, French marigold (*Tagetes*), and morning glory (*Ipomoea*). Plants are available from early to mid May. Plant them in 9 cm (3½ in) pots. Trailing kinds, such as petunias, can be planted in hanging baskets and hung from the greenhouse roof where they make a spectacular display. Climbers, such as morning glory, can either be planted in hanging baskets, where they climb up the chains as well as dangling over the sides, or they can be planted in large pots with twiggy sticks for support.

Cultivation Plant the bulbs in half pots of normal potting compost in autumn, with their tips just showing above the compost. Space them close together, so that the bulbs are almost touching. Keep them in a cool dark place, such as the foot of a north-facing wall, or in the back of the garage, until shoots appear, and then place under the greenhouse staging for a week or two while they acclimatize to the light. Move them to the top of the staging when their buds are well developed.

PLANTING SPRING BULBS IN POTS
Cover the drainage hole with crocks and then half fill the pot with compost. Press the bulbs firmly into position, so they are close together but not touching. Fill the pot to within 15 mm (½ in) of the rim.

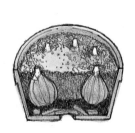

The flamboyant red and orange blooms of tuberous begonias can be relied upon to introduce a splash of colour to the greenhouse in summer. Store the tubers in a dry, frost-free place over winter, and start them into growth again in the warmth the following spring.

After flowering, plant the bulbs out in the garden, or leave them in their pots for next year. If you do keep them in pots, continue watering and feeding the plants regularly until the foliage starts to die away naturally, and then allow the compost to dry out gradually. The bulbs should be kept perfectly dry in summer while they are dormant.

BEGONIA

Tuberous begonias are large, colourful, summer-flowering pot plants, grown from tubers, which are frost tender and need to be dried off and stored indoors overwinter. Buy plants in mid May, or from March onwards. Start tubers into growth on a warm indoor windowsill by laying them hollow side up on a tray of moist potting compost. When shoots start appearing, pot each tuber into a 13 cm (5 in) half pot, with the top of the tuber just visible above the compost.

Move the plants out to the greenhouse after the risk of frost is past, and grow them in slight shade. Pot large specimens on into 18 cm (7 in) pots, and keep them well fed and watered during the summer. Remove dead flowers to encourage new buds to form. Support the plants by tying their stems to split canes if necessary. They will grow to a height of about 30–45 cm (12–18 in). Towards the end of September, when the leaves start turning yellow, gradually reduce the amount of water until the old stems fall off, leaving just the dormant tuber in the pot. Keep this completely dry and in a frost-free place overwinter, away from ice and damp.

BUSY LIZZIE

An easy flowering pot plant that is technically a half-hardy perennial, although it is most conveniently treated as an annual. Busy Lizzies bloom throughout summer; the plants are about 15–20 cm (6–8 in) high, and come in a good range of colours, with single or double flowers. Feed and water the plants well during the summer, and keep them slightly shaded from direct sun. To keep the plants flowering well, regularly remove dead flower heads. Propagate new plants from cuttings taken any time during the summer.

CAMELLIA

Choice, hardy outdoor shrubs which

GROWING BEGONIAS FROM TUBERS

1. Lay the tubers concave-side-up and 5 cm (2 in) apart on dampened potting compost in a seed tray. Press them in lightly, to no more than half their depth.

2. When the shoots appear and two or three leaves have opened out, pot up into 13 cm (5 in) pots so that the top of the tuber is just visible above the compost.

flower very early in the spring, and make spectacular pot plants for growing in large tubs in a cold greenhouse during winter and early spring. Such protection produces a much better display of flowers than you would get outdoors.

Feed and water plants well while they are in bud, and later remove the flower heads when they have died. Place plants back outdoors after flowering, and keep them on the patio in slight shade for the summer. Bring them back under glass in November, ready for flowering. When repotting is required, use some ericaceous compost, and try to water with rainwater or water that has been first boiled in the kettle and then cooled, as camellias are lime-hating plants.

CELOSIA

Half-hardy annual greenhouse pot plants, grown for their striking flowers. There are two different types: cockscomb (*Celosia argentea* 'Cristata') which produces a large, wavy crest of flowers, and Prince of Wales feather (*C. argentea* 'Plumosa'), which has an upright spire of feathery flowers. Both types come in very bright, eye-catching colours, and always attract a lot of attention.

Plants are grown from seed, which should be sown in late spring. If you want early-flowering plants, sow the seeds indoors on a warm windowsill in March. Prick the seedlings out when they are big enough to handle, and later pot the young plants into 9 cm ($3\frac{1}{2}$ in) pots. Young plants and seedlings need shade and moisture, but full-grown plants need more light – shade them from very strong sun though. The plants will continue flowering for about two months. When they are past their best throw the old plants away.

COLEUS

These are half-hardy plants grown for their brilliantly coloured foliage, which makes a superb show all summer long,

Grow camellias in tubs which can be carried into a greenhouse, away from frost, for flowering.

and acts as a good background to flowering plants. The colour range includes purples, reds and yellows, but coleus leaves are usually strongly patterned with different coloured mottles, stripes or spots, and some varieties even have attractively fringed foliage.

Propagation Coleus are grown from seeds sown on a warm indoor windowsill in spring. Seeds are available in a good range of mixtures, but also as individual named varieties. In addition, they can be grown from cuttings, which root easily at any time during the late spring and summer. Pot the seedlings or rooted cuttings into 9 cm ($3\frac{1}{2}$ in) pots; for larger specimens, pot on into 13 cm (5 in) pots.

Keep young plants slightly shaded at first, but older plants tolerate quite bright

31

direct sun, provided they are kept well watered. Coleus plants should be constantly kept just moist, or they soon start to wilt. Feed regularly to maintain good leaf colour. Also, remove any flowers as soon as they start to appear (usually later in the summer) or the leaf colour will fade (you are not missing anything for coleus flowers are not very attractive anyway). At the end of the summer throw the old plants away, unless you have a very warm place indoors where you can keep them during the winter months.

EUCALYPTUS

A very large group of Australian trees, not all of which are hardy, some making good pot plants for the greenhouse. Eucalyptus are grown for their foliage, which in many varieties is an attractive silver-grey colour, and makes a good background for flowering plants. The juvenile foliage of some types is round, and looks like rows of silvery discs threaded together. All the species have scented leaves.

Hardy species such as *E. perriniana*, *E. gunni* and snow gum (*E. niphophila*) may be grown in a cold greenhouse for a few years until they get too big, and then planted out in the garden. Tender species, such as *E. cordatus* and lemon scented gum (*E. citriodora*), can be grown in large pots and cut back every spring to keep

Above: Coleus are half-hardy plants grown for their brightly coloured and patterned foliage. Raise them either from cuttings, or from seed – packets including a mixture with a good range of leaf colours are readily available.

Left: Fuchsias with large blooms are not hardy and must be kept in a frost-free greenhouse over winter. In summer they can be moved outdoors, but if you keep them under glass, make sure ventilation is good and they are shaded from the sun.

them small and bushy. These tender species, however, should be kept indoors as they need frost protection during the winter. Propagation is by seed sown in spring or summer.

FUCHSIA

Showy, frost-tender, flowering shrubs, with characteristic 'skirts' to their flowers. Plants bloom profusely from spring until autumn. A wide range of cultivars are available in a good choice of colours – some also have gold or bronze-orange coloured leaves.

Fuchsias should be moved into the greenhouse in May when the risk of frost is past. Repot old plants, or pot up rooted cuttings taken the previous year into 9 cm ($3\frac{1}{2}$ in) pots. Stop the young plants once or twice to make them bushy. Grow the plants on in lightly shaded, humid conditions, and ventilate the greenhouse well to prevent it from becoming too hot. Keep them regularly fed and well-watered – the compost should be kept just moist throughout the summer.

Towards late September, when the leaves start turning yellow, gradually reduce the amount of watering and stop feeding as plants are preparing for their winter rest. When all the leaves have fallen, give a little water about once a month to lightly moisten the compost and cut the plants back to within 5 cm (2 in) of the top of the pots. Keep them in a frost-free place for winter, hardly ever watering until new growth starts the next spring.

Fuchsias are easily propagated from cuttings taken at any time during the spring and summer. The best flowers are produced by young plants, so if possible propagate new fuchsia plants every year.

GERANIUM

Correctly speaking, these should be called zonal pelargoniums to distinguish them from the true geranium which is a hardy perennial border plant, otherwise known as cranesbill.

Greenhouse geraniums are frost-tender plants that flower from early spring well into the autumn, and are available in all colours except yellow and blue. Plants are available usually from spring onwards – do not put them into an unheated greenhouse until after the risk of serious frost is over, in May. Geraniums like plenty of

Above: The beautiful scarlet blooms of *Fuchsia* 'Thalia' contrast well with its deep bronze-green foliage.

Left: Gloxinias come in varying shades of red, pink, violet and purple, often with a contrasting light or dark centre. They are particularly attractive pot plants for display indoors.

33

sun, and flower best if not over generously fed or watered.

Towards late September the plants will start shedding many of their leaves, which indicates that they are getting ready for their winter rest. When this happens, gradually cut down on watering and stop feeding. Finally cut down the old plants to within 5 cm (2 in) of the top of the pots. During the winter, plants must be kept dry and in a frost-free place, such as an indoor windowsill.

Geraniums are easily propagated from cuttings taken any time from spring to late summer. Bedding geraniums can also be propagated from seeds sown either very early in the spring, or better still in early autumn, to flower the following year. Either way, they must be grown in heat until May – on a warm indoor windowsill, or in a heated propagator. Young plants have a tendency to be leggy, and are best stopped when only several centimetres high to encourage them to produce lots of side shoots and become bushy.

GLOXINIA

Also known as *Sinningia*, these tender perennial plants are grown from corms in much the same way as tuberous begonias. Plants can normally be bought throughout the spring and summer. However, if growing your own, start the corms into growth in a warm place (such as an indoor windowsill) in spring, laying them on top of moist compost until they start to sprout. Be sure to lay them the right way up – the

Geraniums are attractive plants, available in colours ranging from white to many shades of pink and red.

TAKING GERANIUM CUTTINGS
Choose shoots 7·5–10 cm (3–4 in) long, cutting off neatly just below a leaf joint. Remove the leaves from the lower 5 cm (2 in). Plant four or five cuttings in a pot, with the lowest leaves just above the surface.

side which has a slight hollow in the middle is the top.

When shoots start to appear, pot each one individually in a 13 cm (5 in) half pot, with the corms just showing above the top of the compost. Water sparingly to start with, but when the plants are growing well they will need feeding and watering frequently. Move them out to the greenhouse in May after the risk of frost is over, and grow them in a slightly shaded spot. In the autumn, when gloxinia leaves start to turn yellow, gradually reduce the amount of water given until the corms eventually dry out. Store in a frost-free place over winter.

HOUSEPLANTS

During the summer the greenhouse is a useful place to keep indoor houseplants temporarily, after they have finished flowering, or when they are in need of rest and rejuvenation. This treatment is suitable for most perennial houseplants, other than tropical kinds. Good candidates include flaming Katy, Christmas cactus,

fuchsias, geraniums, poinsettia, hydrangea, azalea, winter-flowering begonias, cyclamen and aspidistra. Hardy houseplants, such as fatsia, ivies, and fatshedera, can be kept in the greenhouse in summer, and if necessary in winter too.

Cultivation As a general rule, keep houseplants moist, humid and well shaded while they are in the greenhouse, and don't forget to feed them regularly. In warm weather spray them with water daily to maintain high humidity.

To rejuvenate old houseplants that have become tall and leggy, or which have lost a lot of their leaves, start by pruning them back quite hard. In most cases, they can be cut back to several centimetres above the top of the pot. If less drastic action is called for, cut out untidy or dead shoots and generally reshape the plant.

If the roots are beginning to grow out through the holes in the bottom of the pot, repot into the next size pot using fresh potting compost. While they are recover-

Although hydrangeas are usually thought of as garden shrubs, they also make excellent subjects for a cold greenhouse and are easy to care for, producing masses of showy blooms.

ing from repotting, only water to keep the compost just moist; plants that have been pruned hard will not need much water until new shoots are growing strongly. Feed the plants regularly from then on. Do not forget to move all houseplants (apart from hardy kinds, such as ivy) back into the house by the middle of September when the weather will start getting too cold for them at night.

Special requirements Some kinds of houseplants are extremely fussy. Cyclamen corms, for instance, must be allowed to dry off and have a dormant summer. Azaleas and the Christmas cactus are best put out in a shady spot in the garden during the height of summer, though they can be kept under glass in spring and autumn. Poinsettias are notoriously difficult to keep – cut the old plants back hard when the flowers are over, repot if necessary and keep shaded and on the dry side. They probably won't flower until Easter the following year. (Note: see individual entries for full details of each plant's needs.)

Tropical plants These include foliage plants, such as prayer plant (*Maranta*), figs and rubber plants (*Ficus*), *Dieffenbachia*, etc, which are not suitable for moving out to the greenhouse during the summer because they find it difficult to adjust to the change in conditions. Their leaves will frequently turn yellow or brown, ruining their general appearance.

Annual flowering pot plants Plants such as Persian violet (*Exacum*), cineraria and calceolaria, are not worth moving to the greenhouse after flowering. They will die when they have finished flowering, and should then be thrown away. You can, however, use the greenhouse to raise a new crop of these plants from seeds, which will give you enough to keep both the house and greenhouse well supplied.

HYDRANGEA

These garden shrubs are often grown as flowering houseplants, either indoors or out in the greenhouse. Being hardy, hydrangeas can be grown in an unheated greenhouse all the year round, or you can use the greenhouse to keep hydrangeas normally grown indoors, when they are not in flower. The plants flower in late spring and summer, with large mophead-shaped blooms in pink, blue or mauvish purple.

Hydrangeas are very easy to look after. They need plenty of feeding and watering while they are growing and flowering, between April and September. It is particularly important that they do not dry out when in flower or bud. After flowering, remove the dead blooms, cutting their stems back to within several centimetres of the pot, or to a natural junction with another shoot. Do not cut back new shoots which have not yet flowered, for they will bear next year's blooms. Repot old plants that are pot bound in late autumn or early spring. New plants are easily propagated by cuttings which root any time during the spring and summer.

IVY

Ivies are popular hardy pot plants available in a range of leaf shapes and sizes, including several variegated types. As well as the commoner kinds, a fascinating selection of very unusual varieties is available. You can get ivies with spotted, speckled, curled, crimped, bird's foot or heart-shaped leaves.

Ivies grow very well in the greenhouse, provided you keep them shaded from direct sunlight and spray them with water in warm weather to keep the surrounding air moist. They dislike being too hot, so unless the greenhouse is very well ventilated and shaded in summer, it is a good idea to put ivies outdoors during the hottest months.

Propagate new plants by cuttings, which root easily during the spring and summer, and even early autumn. Pot the rooted cuttings into 9 cm ($3\frac{1}{2}$ in) pots, and repot into 13 cm (5 in) half pots when necessary. Trailing ivies can be trained upwards to save space; insert a split cane into the pot and use plant ties to hold the stems in place.

Ivy makes an excellent decorative climber for the cold greenhouse, provided you can keep it shaded from direct sunlight.

LILIES

Some kinds of lilies are sold in summer as flowering houseplants. They can be planted out in the garden after the flowers are over, or repotted into bigger pots and grown in the greenhouse to flower again the following year. You can also buy lily bulbs in spring; plant them in pots for an excellent greenhouse flower display possibly with a gorgeous scent.

Choice and cultivation The most suitable varieties for growing in pots are those that are nõt too tall – *Lilium speciosum* cultivars are ideal (they mainly have white flowers with red or pink spots); also consider Mid Century hybrids, such as 'Paprika' and 'Enchantment' (which have respectively crimson and orange flowers), and the old favourite *Lilium regale* (fragrant white flowers with a brownish maroon reverse).

Plant the bulbs immediately into any good potting compost. One bulb in a 15 cm (6 in) pot makes an attractive plant on its own, but for an even better display plant a group of three in a 25 cm (10 in) pot. Plant them fairly deep, so there is 5 cm (2 in) of compost over the top of each bulb. Water just enough to slightly moisten the compost, but no more. Keep the newly planted

The lily variety 'Enchantment' is a good choice if you have never grown lilies before, as it is easy to cultivate and will do well in a garden border after flowering in the greenhouse.

Polyanthus, and other very small seeds, should be sown on the surface of the compost. Stand the pot in water until the compost is thoroughly dampened, then place inside a polythene bag to retain the moisture until the seeds have germinated. Secure the bag with an elastic band.

bulbs somewhere cool and shady – you can even stand them outside to start with. When the shoots are 7·5–10 cm (3–4 in) tall, move the pots into the greenhouse but continue to water very sparingly, and keep the plants well ventilated and shaded from strong sun. Plants can be taken indoors when they are in flower, or kept in the greenhouse for summer decoration.

PELARGONIUMS (See Geraniums pages 33 to 34)

POLYANTHUS

Small hardy plants, 20–25 cm (8–10 in) high, that are invaluable for providing a good show of colourful flowers under glass during March and April. The individual flowers are much the same shape as those of primroses, but are produced in large clusters at the top of tall stems.

Polyanthus are available in a very good range of colours including red, blue, maroon, pink, orange and yellow; old fashioned gold-laced polyanthus (with a gold rim around the edge of the petals) are also occasionally sold.

Plants are on sale from early to late spring. They should be kept moist and well shaded from bright sun. They dislike too much heat, and are therefore best placed outdoors over summer. Better still, plant old polyanthus out in the garden after flowering, and grow or buy new plants for the greenhouse the following year – young plants produce much better flowers than old ones.

New plants can be propagated by dividing old clumps, or by sowing seeds in the greenhouse in spring. Sow the seeds on the surface of the compost and do not cover them. Instead, put the pot or tray inside a polythene bag after watering – this will maintain the necessary humidity. After the seeds have germinated take the container out of the bag, but continue to keep

Polyanthus hybrids are availabe in a wide range of colours, including many varieties with contrasting centres or rims to the flowers.

the compost moist all the time – this is important, for seedlings will not recover if they dry out. Keep them very well shaded, even after they are potted, and stand young plants outside for the summer.

PRIMROSES

Primroses are now bred in a large range of colours similar to those of polyanthus, and make very useful and colourful early spring flowering plants, normally about 7·5 cm (3 in) high. They belong to the same family of plants as polyanthus, and need similar conditions – shade, moisture, and not too high temperatures, so again stand them outside in the summer or plant them in the garden after flowering. Propagate by dividing the old clumps, or by sowing seeds in the greenhouse in spring, following the same method as for polyanthus.

VEGETABLES

AUBERGINE

The growth of holidays abroad and our exposure to foreign foods has increased our taste for aubergines. But you don't have to rely on a good greengrocer for a supply, since they can be grown easily in an unheated greenhouse in summer.

Plants are often available in spring.

Alternatively, grow your own in a heated propagator – since the plants are slow growing the seeds must be sown in February or March.

Aubergine plants are short and bushy. The backs of the large grey-green leaves are covered in vicious spines as are the stems of the plants, so take care when handling them.

Cultivation Aubergines are grown in much the same way as tomatoes, except that they do not need to have their side shoots removed, nor do they need training up canes or strings.

Plant from mid to late May, but if the weather is cold delay buying plants until the end of the month, or keep them on an indoor windowsill until the weather improves. Grow the aubergines in a well-prepared greenhouse border, spacing the plants about 75 cm (30 in) apart. They can also be grown in large 30–38 cm (12–15 in) pots, although they will not produce such large crops as they would in a border. Feed the plants immediately after planting with liquid tomato feed (at the manufacturer's recommended rate for tomatoes). Keep the plants well watered throughout the summer.

Plants do not have to be supported, but if required push three 90–120 cm (3–4 ft)

canes in a circle around each plant and tie the branches to them in case they flop. Check the plants regularly for whitefly, red spider mite and greenfly, and spray them if necessary. Grey mould may be troublesome in very damp weather in the autumn, but normally the plants are relatively disease-free.

Cropping Aubergine plants start flowering soon after planting, and their strange purplish flowers are quickly followed by fruits which can be picked as soon as they are big enough to use. They do not need to ripen. The more often you pick, the more aubergines you will get. If you leave fruit on the plants too long they become full of hard seeds and prevent the plants from producing more fruit in the meantime. Plants will continue cropping until the weather gets too cold for them, probably around late September.

CARROTS (EARLY)

You can get a useful crop of early carrots from a sowing made in the border in late February or early March. Sow an early variety such as 'Amsterdam Forcing', 'Chantenay Red Cored', 'Early Scarlet Horn' or 'Nantes' in the border, in rows 22 cm (9 in) apart. Thin the seedlings to 5 cm (2 in) apart when they are big enough,

Aubergines are an unusual yet easily cultivated vegetable for the greenhouse. They require much the same treatment as tomatoes, although it is unnecessary to provide any support unless the branches are in danger of collapsing under the weight of their crop.

and keep the border soil just moist.

The carrots will be ready to pull in late May, in time to plant cucumbers, peppers or aubergines afterwards. Early varieties of carrot can also be sown in the greenhouse border in late August or early September for a late autumn crop of 'early' carrots. Do not allow the soil to dry out or the greenhouse temperature to get too high if growing late crops.

CUCUMBERS

Cucumbers are one of the most productive greenhouse crops you can grow. One plant should be enough to keep a small family supplied with all the cucumbers they can use; grow two to be on the safe side or if you eat lots of cucumber sandwiches!

Cultivation The fruit grow on a long rambling vine-like plant that is normally trained up a cane or string, so that it does not take up too much room. The plants are usually grown in the border or in growing bags, though large 30–38 cm (12–15 in) pots are also suitable.

Plants in the border are easiest to look after, but if you have previously grown cucumbers in the same soil for several years or had plants die from root rot, it is advisable to grow in pots or bags instead. This is because cucumber plants are very susceptible to their own set of root diseases which persist in the soil from one crop to the next. Young plants are available in the spring, but as they are fast growing you can raise your own from seed on a warm indoor windowsill.

Varieties The new F1 hybrid varieties such as 'Diana', 'Monique' and 'Pepinex 69' (which only produce female flowers) are the least trouble to grow, and the above are all especially suitable for cold greenhouses. Alternatively you could grow a good outdoor variety, which does very well under glass especially in a poor summer.

Modern outdoor cucumbers are a great improvement on the old ridge cucumbers which were rather coarse, did not taste good, had a thick skin covered in prickles and lurid yellow stripes and spots! The Japanese outdoor varieties, such as 'Tokyo Slicer' and 'Kyoto' produce normal looking cucumbers, and give excellent crops under glass.

Propagation Cucumber plants can be slightly temperamental to grow in the early stages, so it pays to take special care. If you are growing your own, sow the seeds remembering that they take four weeks to develop into plants.

Sow each seed individually into a 9 cm ($3\frac{1}{2}$ in) pot of seed compost (see Cucumber and Melon Plants, page 72, for details of plant raising). Whether you buy plants or grow your own, it is important to time them just right. They should be ready to plant in late May or early June, just as the plants fill their pots with roots, so sow the seed about 4 weeks earlier. Cucumber plants should not be allowed to get pot bound – if you have to delay planting for any reason, it is better to pot them on into a larger pot. However, if the weather is cold at planting time, wait until it becomes warmer because the cold can check cucumber growth badly – and they take a long time to recover.

The new all-female cucumber varieties are the most straightforward for growing under glass. These healthy young plants are ready for planting out into the greenhouse border, growing bags or large pots. You are unlikely to need as many plants as this, but it is a good idea to grow a few spare plants in case of disasters in the early stages.

GREENHOUSE GARDENING

When planting in the border, space cucumbers about 75 cm (2½ ft) apart. In bags, insert two or three plants in each row, or if using pots, plant in 30–38 cm (12–15 in) size containers filled with good potting compost. Water in lightly after planting, but be very careful not to water any more than you need for the first two or three weeks while the plants are developing a good root system.

During this time they are liable to rot off if the soil is too damp. Instead, spray the leaves once or twice on a fine day, which

These cucumbers are ready for harvesting, as they have reached the right thickness – do not leave them on the plant to grow larger, as the flavour deteriorates and the plant will stop producing new fruits.

MALE AND FEMALE CUCUMBER FLOWERS

Male flowers (above right) are attached to the plant with a short stalk, while female flowers (below right) are produced at the end of a miniature cucumber. The male flowers should be removed as soon as possible to prevent them pollinating the female flowers, resulting in bitter, inedible fruits.

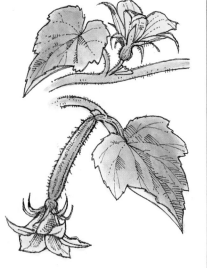

helps to keep the air around the plants humid (put your thumb over the end of the hose to produce a fine spray). It is also a good idea to damp down the whole greenhouse daily by spraying the floor as an additional means of creating humidity.

Providing support As the plants start to grow they will need support. You can either grow them up canes or strings. If using canes, place a 1·5–1·8 m (5–6 ft) cane alongside each plant, and tie the stem to it with twist ties or thick string (thin string can cut into the stems, causing damage).

If you prefer to grow the plants up strings, they should be put in place before planting the cucumbers. Again, use very thick string reaching from the roof to the floor of the greenhouse, with about 30 cm (12 in) over. Make planting holes for the cucumbers, and fix one string to a hook in the roof of the greenhouse above each

planting hole. Then when you plant, bury the bottom of the string underneath the root ball of each cucumber. To hold the stem upright, you just twist it round the string every few days as the plant grows.

Troubleshooting Besides keeping the main stem of the plants upright, there are also side shoots to be dealt with. (These are small shoots growing out from the main stem of the plant in the junction where a leaf stalk joins the main stem.) The way to handle these side shoots depends on whether you are growing all-female cucumber varieties.

With all-female varieties, the cucumber fruits are produced in the leaf joints, along with the side shoots. So with these varieties you should remove all the side shoots every few days, nipping them off between thumb and forefinger while they are still small. Take great care, when side

shooting, not to remove the tiny baby cucumbers by mistake – it's easily done.

If growing varieties other than all-female, the technique has to be slightly different because here, cucumbers are not grown in the leaf joints, but only on side shoots. Therefore, leave the side shoots to grow until they produce cucumbers.

Normally, each side shoot will produce one cucumber by the time it has grown about four to six leaves. As soon as a cucumber has formed, stop the shoot by pinching out its growing tip one leaf beyond the developing fruit. To complicate matters slightly, this group of cucumbers does not just produce female flowers (the ones that become cucumbers) but male flowers too. It is important to remove all the male flowers as soon as they appear, otherwise the cucumber fruits will be pollinated. This makes them virtually inedible, as they become bitter and eventually fill up with hard seeds.

You can always tell when a cucumber has been pollinated because it swells up at one end – growers call them 'bee stung' cucumbers. Incidentally, it isn't difficult to tell male and female flowers apart. Male flowers have only a short stalk behind them, whereas female flowers have a quite distinct small baby cucumber at the back of them.

Harvesting Once the plants are growing strongly, increase the amount of water and start feeding regularly with a general-purpose liquid or soluble plant food, following the manufacturer's instructions. Continue spraying the plants and damping down the greenhouse daily whenever it is warm, and start picking cucumbers as soon as they fill out all the way along their length.

Pick regularly and cut off the cucumbers at the stalk with secateurs or a sharp knife. If you leave fruit on the plants to get bigger, the flavour deteriorates and the plants stop producing new cucumbers until the mature fruit have been cut.

Pests and diseases Watch for greenfly and whitefly, and spray when necessary, checking with the instructions that the chemical is suitable for cucumbers, because many products are not. Where possible, use one that allows treated crops to be eaten within a day or two of spraying.

Towards the end of the summer, around early September, cucumber plants are often affected by powdery mildew which looks like talcum powder on the tops of the leaves, so spray with benomyl. Then, as the weather begins to get cold at night, the plants will be more severely affected by mildew and will also stop producing more cucumbers. When this happens, cut the last of the crop and pull out the plants.

FIGS

When they are grown outside in the garden, figs take up a great deal of room and rarely produce much ripe fruit. If you live in the north of the country, you are unlikely to get any at all. By growing a potted fig in the greenhouse, however, you can get a good crop of ripe fruit from a plant only about 90 cm (3 ft) tall.

The ordinary outdoor varieties such as 'Brunswick' and 'Brown Turkey' can be grown under glass, but you can buy varieties especially for growing in greenhouses, such as 'White Marseilles', 'Negro Largo', etc, which bear better flavoured fruit than outdoor figs.

Cultivation Fig plants are easy to grow. In spring select a bushy young plant. Put it into a larger pot if the roots are starting to grow out through the holes in the bottom of the old container, and use John Innes potting compost No. 3.

As new growth begins, do not water much to start with until the plant has produced several new leaves. As the summer progresses, you will gradually need to increase the amount of water. By the time small figs start to appear at the tips of the shoots, the plant will need quite heavy watering.

It is vital to keep the compost evenly moist from this stage onwards, as the developing fruit will drop off if the plant is allowed to get dry. On hot sunny days, up to $4\frac{1}{2}$ litres (1 gallon) of water a day may be needed. Figs also need extensive feeding during this time.

Harvesting The fruit will start ripening towards late summer. You can tell if it is ripe by gently squeezing the figs. If they are very soft, and the skin splits open easily, or the fruit falls off into your hand, they are ready to eat. This is also the time when purple-skinned figs develop their distinctive colour. Not all the figs will ripen at once, for the crop comes to fruition over about four to six weeks. Pick them regularly.

Not long after the last fig has ripened, the leaves start to turn yellow and fall off. This is a sign that the plant is preparing for its winter rest, and you should therefore gradually reduce the amount of water given. By the time all the leaves have dropped off, stop watering altogether. The plant can be kept completely dry throughout the winter months.

Pruning The plants need to be pruned to stop them from growing too big. This should be done in winter when they are dormant. Cut the main branches back by about half or a third, and cut out any that are crossing, badly placed or which have grown too close together.

Growing figs in pots under glass is a reliable way of producing a good harvest of ripe fruit. Gently squeeze the figs to see if they are ripe – they should feel very soft and should easily come off in your hand. Purple-skinned figs develop their distinctive colour as they ripen.

Aim for a pleasing overall shape within which branches are well spaced out round the trunk, and not crossing or touching each other.

However, if you prefer, you can summer prune instead. This is the best method, since it makes the plant grow very slowly keeping it compact and bushy, which means it can produce more fruit. It is a bit more trouble than winter pruning though. First, establish the basic shape of the plant in winter, either as a low bush, or short standard, by cutting out surplus shoots with sharp secateurs. Then, in spring when the plant starts to grow, allow each shoot to produce four full-sized leaves, and then nip out the very tip of the growing point. Side shoots will grow which in turn must be stopped after they have produced four full-sized leaves. Keep doing this every time new shoots are produced, and you will have a very neat, compact and fruitful miniature fig tree. If you want more plants, they can easily be propagated from cuttings taken any time during the summer.

Each year as fig plants start growing in the spring, repot them into larger pots, using John Innes potting compost No. 3. However, when they end up in 33–45 cm (15–18 in) pots eventually, it is clearly not practical to keep moving them into bigger containers. Instead top dress by scraping away the top layer of compost, replacing it with fresh matter.

GRAPES

Grapes are another crop that traditionally take up a lot of room, and one vine can easily dominate the entire greenhouse. The best means of keeping a vine compact is by growing it in a pot, although this will produce a smaller crop.

Cultivation   A pyramid is probably the most suitable shape for training a pot-grown vine. It takes up least space and produces most fruit.

Start with a pot-grown vine in spring. Make sure you buy a greenhouse variety rather than the sort sold for growing out of doors, whose fruit will normally only be suitable for making into wine. Garden centres often sell vines such as 'Black Hamburgh', for growing under glass. Repot the young plant into a larger pot using John Innes potting compost No. 3, and

Training a vine so that it produces heavy bunches of ripe grapes is a long and careful process, but after about three years you can expect a delicious crop like this every summer. A well-pruned pot-grown plant is the most fruitful and convenient for a small greenhouse – left to itself a vine will soon take over the entire greenhouse.

begin training it straight away. Each spring, repot it into a larger pot. Eventually it will need a 38–45 cm (15–18 in) pot, after which you should only provide a new top dressing each year, as with figs. As growth commences, gradually increase the watering and also begin feeding the plant again.

Forming the shape   The first year will be spent getting the vine properly established and growing it into the right shape, so unfortunately there won't be any fruit at this stage. Using secateurs, cut back the vine to within about 15 cm (6 in) of the top of the pot, cutting just above a leaf joint.

When the shoots start to grow out from the base of the plant, select the strongest three, ensuring they are well spaced out round the plant. Rub the rest out by gently picking them off with your fingers, and removing them flush with the main stem of the plant.

Push three 1·5–1·8 m (5–6 ft) canes in around the edge of the pot (next to each shoot) and tie them together at the top to form a tripod. As the three main shoots grow, train each one up its own cane, tying it in place at regular intervals with soft string or raffia. When the stems are 1·5 m (5 ft) high, stop them by pinching out the growing point. If any side shoots develop, allow them to grow two or three leaves and then pinch out their growing points too. This will build up a strong framework which forms the basis of your plant for future years.

Feeding   Keep the young vine well fed and watered while it is growing strongly, using general-purpose liquid or soluble feed. In the autumn, when the leaves start to turn yellow, gradually cut down the amount of water until the leaves have all fallen off and the compost feels almost completely dry when you touch it.

The vine will remain dormant over winter, during which time it should not be watered at all.

Pruning Each winter cut down each stem to about 20 cm (8 in) from the point where it branches out from the main trunk.

Training As before, select the strongest three shoots (one from each of the three stumps you have left from last year), and train them up the three canes. They will produce a few flowers and some fruit in the second year, but you should get better crops after that. It is specially important the vine does not dry out or go short of feed when flowers or fruit are present. At the end of the year, after the leaves have fallen from the vine, prune it back as before, leaving just three short stubs at the base.

If you cannot be bothered to train and prune a vine properly you could just let it scramble up wire netting or a trellis. How-ever, this method will produce a lot of tangled shoots and foliage, and not much fruit. It is also something of a health hazard, for it spreads over all the greenhouse, preventing you keeping it clean.

HERBS

In summer, herbs grow so well outside that there is little point in having them in the greenhouse. But towards late summer they stop growing and by autumn even the perennial kinds, such as chives and mint, start to die down for the winter. This is when it is valuable to have a supply of fresh herbs growing under glass. Even in a cold house you can keep herbs going for several months after they would have died down outdoors.

Transfer under glass Dig up clumps of chives, parsley, and marjoram in September, choose pots that comfortably hold all their roots with a bit of room to spare, and pot them up. If you have evergreen herbs, such as sage, rosemary or thyme growing in pots on the patio, move them into the greenhouse too. This saves their leaves from being browned by the frost.

Mint roots can also be dug up from the garden in winter, any time between November and February, and forced into growth early in the cold greenhouse. Half fill a seed tray with compost, and spread the roots out on it. Cover them with several centimetres of compost, and water lightly. If you have a heated propagator, a week or two inside with the temperature set at 16°–21°C (60–70°F) will provide an excellent start. Avoid overwatering herbs in the greenhouse during winter, and remove dead leaves regularly.

LETTUCE

It is not worth trying to grow lettuces in the greenhouse in summer as it is much easier to have them outside in the garden. But if you want lettuce for Christmas or early spring, before the garden crops are ready, then the only way is by growing them under glass, in the greenhouse border.

Problems Winter lettuce is not very easy to grow. The naturally poor growing conditions at that time of year make the plants terribly susceptible to grey mould and other fungal diseases, so it is very important to take great care with the crop.

It is also important to choose the right varieties for growing under glass in winter – you can't use the same sort you sow outside in summer. Unlike summer lettuce, which can be sown over a long period of time, winter lettuce must be sown at precisely the right time, which will differ with each variety. The seed packets always specify these sowing times, so follow the instructions.

Varieties Good choices for unheated greenhouses include: 'Kwiek', a traditional round lettuce sown in August to cut in time for Christmas; 'Marmer', a compact iceberg type lettuce sown in late August or early September for cutting early in the New Year; 'Plus', another round lettuce, sown in October or November for cutting in April and 'Kelly's', an iceberg type sown from November to January, for cutting from the end of April and early May. In February and March you can sow the

With care lettuces can be grown in the greenhouse border to provide a welcome supply of salad leaves in the winter months. They should be planted about 20 cm (8 in) apart and it is a good idea to grow rows of different varieties to obtain the longest possible cropping period.

outdoor variety 'Little Gem', a miniature cos lettuce with a superb taste, to grow in the greenhouse for cutting in May. For continuity of cropping, try growing a row each of several different varieties.

Sowing and growing Sow the seeds very thinly in a pot. Later, when the seedlings are big enough to handle, prick them out into small individual peat pots filled with seed compost. Plant as soon as the first roots start to appear through the sides of the pot (remember that when using peat pots the roots grow straight through the sides so you must plant 'pot and all').

Space the lettuces about 20 cm (8 in) apart. Do not plant them too deeply; ideally the edges of the peat pots should stand about 13 mm ($\frac{1}{2}$ in) above soil level when they are planted. Water the plants well in, but from then on try to avoid watering any more than is absolutely essential. Test by pushing a finger down into the soil and if it feels really dry then water again. Water in the morning so the foliage is dry by night time. Water again when the plants have grown so big that they are just touching each other. Then,

unless they start wilting, try not to water again. This is the point when mildew and rotting is most likely to occur. Spray with a fungicide the minute you see any disease, or it spreads like wildfire.

Lettuce is ready to cut once a small heart has formed. The winter types do not form such big hearts as summer outdoor types, and are generally much smaller lettuces anyway, so don't wait too long. Since winter lettuce is such a tricky crop to grow, and the lettuces are not as good as the summer types, lots of people avoid the problem by growing an easier winter crop as the basis for winter salads. Raw spinach leaves or corn salad, for instance, are both far tastier and easier to grow.

MELONS

Melons are close relatives of cucumbers. The plants look almost identical until they start bearing fruit, and they are similar to grow although there are one or two important differences.

Varieties The plants are grown from seed sown in spring, in exactly the same way as described for cucumbers. Plants can usually be bought around May. There

are three different basic families of melons: musk melons (which are the old hot-house kind); watermelons (which also need a heated greenhouse to grow well); and canteloupe melons. Canteloupes are the kind to choose for growing in an unheated greenhouse. Of these, the best variety by far is 'Sweetheart', which will give you lots of ripe melons even in a poor summer. 'Sweetheart' melons are small, with a green rind and beautifully scented salmon-pink flesh inside. The flavour is superb. Other good varieties include 'Gaylia' (yellow netted rind with green flesh), 'Blenheim Orange' (cream netted rind with red flesh) and 'Ogen' (orange and beige striped rind with greenish-yellow flesh).

Cultivation Plant melons under glass in late May, either in the border, in growing bags, or in large pots as for cucumbers (see page 39). If planting in the border, it is a good idea to pile some soil up into a mound about 15 cm (6 in) high and plant into the top of that. This makes excess water drain away quickly from around the roots, and helps prevent them from rotting.

Water sparingly at first and damp over

Melons are grown in much the same way as cucumbers, and canteloupe varieties are ideal for a cold greenhouse. Unlike cucumbers, the flowers must be pollinated or fruit will fail to develop. Restrict the fruit to three or four per plant and if you are training the plants upwards remember to support the fruit with netting unless you are growing a small fruited variety such as 'Sweetheart'.

frequently as suggested for cucumbers. But when plants start growing strongly they will need more water and regular feeding. It is better to feed little and often rather than risk scorching the roots by giving the plants a solution of feed which is far too strong.

Training Cantaloupe plants can either be allowed to ramble over the ground, without any training or pruning, or you can train them up canes just like cucumbers. Although you will get a good crop by just letting them ramble, they take up a lot of room. Also because they are laying on the ground, you will need to protect them from slugs and from rotting. Do this by lifting developing fruit up off the ground, resting them on tiles to prevent them from rotting. Remember to scatter slug pellets regularly around the plants.

Growing melons up canes takes up less room than if they are left to ramble over the ground, and makes it easier to control pests such as greenfly and whitefly. To grow cantaloupe melons up canes, train them in exactly the same way as the cucumbers that are not 'all-female' flowering. Train the main stem of the plant up the cane, tying it in place at 2·5 cm (1 in) intervals with soft string or raffia.

Remove all side shoots from the lower 45 cm (18 in) of stem, and allow them to grow out above this height until they have produced a female flower (which is recognizable by the tiny baby melon just behind it). Stop the side shoot one leaf beyond the developing fruit, to encourage the fruit to swell to a good size.

Pollination Unlike cucumbers, melons must be pollinated or they do not set any fruit. If you leave the door open during the day, bees may find their way into the greenhouse and do the job of pollination for you.

But if you want to guarantee pollination occurs every time, you will need to hand pollinate to do this. Find a female flower that has just opened and pick a male flower (which has a short stem behind it, and no small melon). Then remove its petals, and gently dab the centre of the male flower into the middle of the female flower. Do this every day or two, and it should ensure a good crop. As the fruits swell, remove any that are unusually

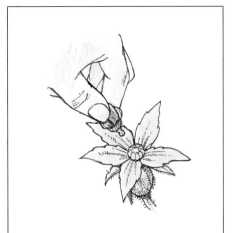

Although in the right conditions bees will pollinate your melon flowers, it is safer to hand pollinate them. Pick a fully-opened male flower, remove the petals and dab into the centre of a female flower. For the best results, treat all the female flowers that are open every day in this way.

large, or they will continue to grow at the expense of the rest.

If you want to grow melons and cucumbers together in the same greenhouse, it is important to keep bees out of the greenhouse as they will pollinate all-female cucumbers with pollen from melons. To prevent this from happening, attach fine netting over the ventilators and drape it over the doorway, and pollinate the melons by hand.

Harvesting Once the melons have been pollinated, they swell up fast and need much more feeding and watering than before. The first melons will normally start ripening around July or early August in a warm summer.

You can tell when one is ripe the moment you walk into the greenhouse, because of the sweet musky scent. Also, the ripe melon will have changed colour slightly, and if you gently press the end of the fruit furthest from the stalk, you'll find it slightly 'gives'. A melon should come away easily from the plant when you lift it.

Canteloupes will keep ripening in succession until the weather gets too cold for them in early autumn. Any fully grown fruit still on the plants by then may ripen in a warm shady place indoors. Pull the old plants out when all the fruit has been picked, and no more new fruit are setting.

PEPPERS
Sweet peppers are now available in supermarkets in a wide range of colours; orange, purple and yellow, as well as the familiar green and red. In addition to the more usual squarish shaped peppers you can also get long pointed kinds, sometimes called 'banana' peppers, and the fiery hot chilli peppers.

You can usually buy plants of ordinary green and red peppers in the spring. If you want the unusual kinds you will have to grow your own from seed.

Sowing and growing To raise your own plants you need a heated greenhouse and ideally a propagator, though you can often get by with a warm indoor windowsill. Sow the seeds in March, three or four to a 9 cm ($3\frac{1}{2}$ in) pot, and pull out all but the strongest seedling when they develop, leaving just one plant to grow in each pot.

Peppers are ready to plant when the pot is full of roots. In a cold greenhouse, plant the peppers from mid May to mid June when the weather turns warm. They are not difficult to grow, being cultivated in exactly the same way as aubergines. The plants are similar in habit to aubergines – low growing and bushy – but unlike aubergines they do not have any spines.

Harvesting If you want green peppers, they are ready to pick as soon as they are large enough to use – you don't have to wait for them to ripen. If you want red, purple, orange or yellow peppers, you will have to leave them on the plants until they ripen – they are green or creamy green to start with, and their colour only develops when they ripen. However, this takes quite a long time and while they are ripening the plants don't produce any more peppers. This means that your total crop will be very much smaller if you want ripe fruits. So just grow a few extra plants to keep up your supply.

POTATOES (EARLY)
Very early new potatoes are not only delicious, they are very easy to grow in a cold greenhouse. What's more, they also produce a good crop. Choose an early variety such as 'Duke of York', 'Epicure',

'Chit' seed potatoes for forcing by standing them in a seed tray, eye end uppermost, in a cool dark place indoors. They are ready for planting when the shoots are 3–5 cm ($1\frac{1}{4}$–2 in) long. Don't wait too long, or the shoots will become weak and spindly, and will not grow so quickly once planted out.

Potatoes are an excellent vegetable for forcing under glass, as they are easy to grow and produce a good crop. Buy the seed potatoes as early as possible – preferably in early February – and be sure to choose an early variety like these well-grown Pentland Javelin potatoes.

'Maris Bard', 'Pentland Javelin', 'Sharpe's Express' or 'Sutton's Foremost'.

Starting from seed Buy seed potatoes for forcing under glass as early as you can get them, if possible, in early February. Set the seed potatoes to sprout in a cool dark place indoors. Then stand them in a seed tray with all the 'eyes' uppermost. When the potatoes have sprouts about 2·5–5 cm (1–2 in) long, they are ready for planting.

Cultivation Plant in the border soil spacing them about 2·5 cm (1 in) apart. Alternatively, you can grow them in pots or growing bags. If so, you can move the plants outside if you later need space in the greenhouse, but you won't get such a big crop as you would from the border.

Water sparingly until the foliage is growing vigorously. Feeding is not necessary if you applied Growmore when preparing the soil before planting. When the foliage is about 45 cm (18 in) high, the first potatoes should be ready.

Harvesting There is no need to dig up the plants; feel around in the top layers of soil surrounding each plant and you will be able to pick the first harvest of baby new potatoes.

After you have picked over all the plants in this way, two or three times, dig up the plants a few at a time and gather the rest of the crop as you need them. Early potatoes grown in the border will have

been harvested in time to plant summer crops such as cucumbers, peppers and aubergines.

Potatoes grown in pots and growing bags can be moved outside to make room for, perhaps, earlier planted tomatoes from the end of April.

RADISH

Radishes are a fast growing crop and they take up little room. This makes them a very productive way of filling any odd gaps between rows of other slower growing crops. They can be sown, for instance, between newly planted rows of tomatoes, cucumbers, peppers or aubergines, early spring-sown carrots or turnips.

For the best results, choose a variety of radish specially intended for growing early under glass, such as 'Ribella', 'Cherry Belle' or 'Saxa Short Top'. These

can be sown in a cold greenhouse in spring from February until late April, and again in early autumn for a late crop.

Sow thickly in rows allowing at least 10–13 cm (4–5 in) between surrounding crops, and thin to 5 cm (2 in) apart when the seedlings are large enough. Pull individual radishes as soon they are big enough to eat, leaving the rest to grow on. Don't leave in the ground too long.

SPINACH

A very fast maturing crop, handy for making good use of any empty rows in the greenhouse border in early spring or autumn. The leaves can be cooked or used raw in salads.

Choose a summer-cropping variety of spinach such as 'Symphony' or 'Monarch' for spring sowing, and later in the year use a variety specially recommended for autumn sowing such as 'Norvak'. Sow thickly in rows 15–20 cm (6–8 in) apart, and thin in several stages. The thinnings can be used in salads. If large leaves are required, thin seedlings to 15 cm (6 in) apart: if they are left 2·5–5 cm (1–2 in) apart, you will get much smaller leaves.

Protect the plants from slugs as they grow. When the leaves are large enough, begin regular pickings. Finally, pull the plants out when space is needed for other crops, or when the spinach plants start going to seed.

SPRING ONIONS

Spring onions are slow growing, but you can get a worthwhile crop from a small space. Sow seeds of the variety 'White Lisbon' in rows 20 cm (8 in) apart in the border. Seeds sown in early February will give spring onions ready to pull in early June; sow in autumn for an earlier spring crop. Sow thickly, and thin the seedlings out using them for salads.

STRAWBERRIES (EARLY)

Early strawberries are a very productive crop for a cold greenhouse. The plants only occupy the greenhouse for a few months in late winter and early spring, leaving space for summer crops the rest of the time. Early varieties such as 'Cambridge Vigour', 'Grandee', or 'Red Gauntlet' are the best for forcing, though you will get earlier fruit than usual from any variety of strawberry grown under glass.

Cultivation Start to grow strawberries in late summer or early autumn with new plants – which should be potted into 13 cm (5 in) pots on delivery, or use runners from your own fruit garden. These should be pegged down into 9 cm ($3\frac{1}{2}$ in) pots of good compost while still attached to the parent plant, and encouraged to root. When well rooted, cut the runner and move the pots outdoors where you can look after them. Pot them on into 13 cm (5 in) pots when necessary.

To obtain strawberry plants for forcing in the greenhouse propagate from runners on plants outside. Peg the runners into 9 cm ($3\frac{1}{2}$ in) pots of compost in mid to late summer, and cut the connecting stems when the young plants are well rooted.

Radishes are a useful crop for making your greenhouse as productive as possible, as they grow quickly and can be planted in between other, slower growing crops. Sown in early spring or the autumn, they will provide fresh salad vegetables when little else is available in the vegetable garden.

TOMATOES

They are the number one cold greenhouse crop. Many different varieties of tomatoes are available and it is largely a matter of personal choice which you grow.

Varieties Old favourites such as 'Ailsa Craig' and 'Alicante' are still considered among the best for flavour, while many people prefer the heavy cropping 'Moneymaker'. 'Beefsteak' tomatoes, large often ugly shaped fruit of the sort found in Spain, are available in this county now; 'Marmande' is very much like the Spanish tomatoes, while 'Dombo' and 'Dombello' are the same shape as normal tomatoes but very much bigger.

These two varieties are particularly interesting because they lack the unpleasant hard core often found in many beefsteak tomatoes. Also very popular now are 'cherry' tomatoes – varieties such as 'Gardener's Delight' and 'Sweet 100' – which have very tiny, bite-sized fruit with a particularly superb flavour.

Yellow tomatoes, though less well known, also have a very good flavour – try 'Yellow Perfection', or the orange and yellow striped 'Tigerella'. Also worth considering are modern tomatoes, specially bred for disease resistance. If you have experienced problems with root disease in tomatoes and do not want the bother of changing the border soil or growing in bags, try the variety 'Piranto'. There is also a trend towards low bush tomatoes that do not need all the staking, training and side shooting required by normal tomatoes. Of these, 'Tornado' is exceptionally well flavoured. Many of these varieties are available as young plants in spring. Don't be put off if some are described as outdoor tomatoes – they will grow even better in a cold greenhouse.

Growing from seed You need a lot of heat and an early start to grow your own tomato plants. Sow three to four seeds to each 9 cm ($3\frac{1}{2}$ in) pot in February or early March, and thin out to leave only the strongest seedling. Keep the plants growing in pots until the first flower has opened (this method avoids plants with abundant leaves but few tomatoes).

Cultivation Plant tomatoes in a cold greenhouse from the third week in April in

Leave the young plants out of doors for the first part of winter, choosing a north facing spot where the roots will get a good chilling. In January, move them into the greenhouse. Stand them on the staging, and protect from slugs and mice. When they start growing, gradually begin watering and feeding with a general-purpose liquid or soluble feed, but be very careful not to overwater or the plants may rot.

Fruiting When the first flowers appear, pollinate them with a soft artist's brush. This is necessary because it is too early in the season for large numbers of pollinating insects to do the job for you.

To hand pollinate, dab the brush gently into the centre of all the open flowers. Later, when the fruit starts setting, keep the compost in the pots just moist and shade the plants from strong sun on very bright days. Ventilate the greenhouse well

To obtain a good crop of forced strawberries you must start with new plants every year. Allow the fruit to become completely ripe before picking, so that the full flavour develops. Do not force the same plants twice – your second crop will be disappointing.

when the weather is warm so the temperature does not get too high, otherwise the plants may be scorched.

Leave the fruit to ripen fully on the plants so they develop their full flavour, and continue feeding regularly while you are picking to encourage further flowering and fruiting. When all the fruit have been picked, the plants can be put out in the garden to fruit again next year. Do not force the same plants twice, as they won't give such a good crop second time round – instead, raise new plants from runners each year.

2. Tie the top of each plant to its cane regularly, to keep up with the rate at which it is growing. Don't tie too tightly, as the stem will swell as the plant grows.

CULTIVATING TOMATOES

1. Plant tomatoes in tubs, growing bags or the greenhouse border when the first truss of flowers is just starting to open. This prevents the plants growing leafy and unproductive.

3. Pinch out the side shoots (unless you are growing a bush variety) before they grow too large, taking care not to remove any flower trusses by mistake. When the plant reaches the roof of the greenhouse, pinch out the growing tip.

Yellow tomatoes, like 'Yellow Perfection' shown here, are unusual and attractive, and their fruit is of excellent flavour.

a mild season and in the south of the country. If the weather is cold or you live in the north, wait for mid or late May. After planting, water the plants in with a solution of liquid tomato feed diluted to the normal strength, and then keep them distinctly dryish. For the first two weeks, water them sparingly – just enough to prevent them from wilting.

Meanwhile, push a tall cane in alongside each plant for support and, as it grows, tie the main stem to the cane every 20–30 cm (8–12 in) with soft string. Remove all the side shoots as soon as you see them, taking care not to snap off the top of the plant by mistake.

If you are growing bush varieties, don't tie plants up or remove the side shoots. Instead, just use two or three short canes and some string to keep the plants off the ground, as for peppers and aubergines. As the plants grow, water them sparingly until the bottom truss (bunch) of tomatoes has set and you can see the small fruit just starting to swell.

Feeding and watering It is important to both feed and water the plants regularly. From the time the first fruit start swelling, increase both feeding and

49

watering in order to keep pace with both the larger number of leaves and the developing tomatoes.

Try to keep the compost or soil moist all the time to prevent problems such as blossom end rot, or split fruit, from occurring later. This is particularly important with plants growing in pots or growing bags, which dry out much faster than those growing in the border. Spray the plants over with water from a hosepipe on warm days to help the fruit to set (putting your finger over the end will produce a fine, gentle spray).

Harvesting The first tomatoes should start ripening when the plants are around 1·2–1·5 m (4–5 ft) tall. By then they will be carrying a large crop of unripe fruit. At this stage they will need watering every day and feeding frequently, otherwise you will not achieve maximum cropping from your plants.

When the first tomatoes start changing colour, leave them to ripen fully on the plants for maximum flavour. To pick them, snap them off at the knuckle, a natural kink in the short stem attaching the fruit to the plants. Bend up against the direction of the knuckle and the tomatoes will come away complete with their green calyx (sepals) round the top – picked this way they will keep longer than if just pulled from the plant.

Do not be tempted to remove any leaves from the bottom of the plant to speed up ripening because this can spoil the flavour of the tomatoes and lead to them being scorched by the sun. Only remove lower leaves when they have turned yellow, which happens naturally as they age – it does not mean there is anything wrong with the plants.

Problems If all the leaves turn yellowish, it may be a sign that the plants are not being fed enough. In this case, feed them

'Sweet 100', like all cherry tomatoes, has a particularly intense flavour. The heavily-cropping trusses of fruit must be harvested regularly to keep the plant producing tomatoes for as long as possible. The plants must also be fed and watered regularly so that the trusses forming at the top of the plant have a chance to develop fully.

more often while using the same strength solution as usual.

Also watch out for whitefly and greenfly, the commonest pests of tomatoes, and spray when necessary. Use a product which allows you to eat treated crops within a day or two of them being sprayed, since once tomatoes start ripening you will have some ready to pick almost every day.

Early autumn Around mid August to early September, encourage the remaining green tomatoes to ripen before the plants are killed off by cold autumn weather. To do this, first stop the plants. Remove the growing tips of the main stems one leaf beyond the last truss of small green fruit that is just starting to swell.

Also start reducing the amount of water you give the plants (they won't need so much now anyway since much of the crop will have been picked, and the weather is cooler). In addition, you can stop feeding altogether because the plants will soon be pulled out. Remove some of the leaves, particularly on bush tomatoes, to let the weaker sun into the plants to help ripen the remaining fruit.

Six to eight weeks later, stop watering altogether, and after a few more days cut through the base of the stems just above ground level. Leave the plants hanging from their canes. This works wonders, and will ripen up most of the remaining fullsized green fruit.

Just before pulling out the plants, strip all the remaining large green tomatoes from the plants and put them in a cool, darkish place indoors, where they should ripen within two weeks. You can speed up the process by shutting them in a box or drawer with some ripening apples; the ethylene gas given off by the apples helps to ripen the tomatoes. (The traditional way of ripening green tomatoes, on a warm sunny windowsill, makes them shrivel very quickly.) Any tomatoes that do not ripen within two weeks should be thrown away.

If the old tomato crop can be pulled out and the greenhouse given its thorough annual clean before the middle of September, there will be time and space to sow a crop of autumn salads or other fast maturing vegetables. This will probably be more productive than leaving the tomatoes until they are killed by the frost, because as the temperature begins to drop very few new tomatoes will develop – and even if there are any, they will take a long time to ripen.

TURNIPS

Another very useful quick crop that makes profitable use of a spare row or two in the border in early spring. Turnips can also be sown between newly planted rows of tomatoes, peppers or aubergines, which take time to fill all their allotted space.

Choose a fast maturing variety suitable for use when very small, such as 'Tokyo Cross', 'Snowball', or 'Milan White Forcing'. Sow thinly in rows 15–20 cm (6–8 in) apart, and thin when the seedlings are big enough, leaving them 10 cm (4 in) apart.

Apply a soil insecticide to prevent larvae from spoiling the roots. Keep the soil just moist – there is no need to feed this crop. Start pulling turnips as soon as they are the size of golf balls; they will be tender and more flavoursome when small.

Left: If you grow tomatoes in the greenhouse border dig plenty of garden compost or manure into the soil each year, to provide the plants with a rich growing medium.

Above: 'Snowball' is a good variety of turnip for the cold greenhouse, and its tender white roots are best harvested when they are still quite small – the size of golf balls.

PLANTS FOR THE HEATED GREENHOUSE

If you have a greenhouse that can be kept free of frost in winter, or better still at around 4·5°C (40°F), the scope of your growing activities increases enormously. For a start you can try all the plants you could grow in a cold house, but earlier and more easily. You can also grow frost-tender plants such as geraniums and fuchsias in quantity, as you no longer need to restrict yourself to numbers that can be housed on an indoor windowsill in winter. But best of all, a slightly heated greenhouse makes it possible to grow many fascinating plants which it is only really feasible to keep there, including some delightful collector's plants.

ORNAMENTAL PLANTS

AZALEA

Indoor azaleas (*Azalea indica*) are not ideal plants for greenhouse cultivation because they like a steady temperature of 10°–16°C (50–60°F) and moist, shady growing conditions. Also note that when the flowers are over, the plants can be kept for another year if they are temporarily placed in the greenhouse.

Azaleas aren't the easiest of plants to keep, let alone to get to flower again the following year. If you decide to have a go, they need special care. After flowering, remove the dead flower heads, and spray the plants with a systemic fungicide as protection against grey mould. Keep the plants just moist but not saturated, and shade them from direct sun.

In April, pot them carefully into new pots only slightly larger than the previous ones (this is important), using lime-free or ericaceous compost. From time to time give a weak liquid feed, and it also pays to use an occasional foliar feed, such as one based on seaweed. In addition, use a spray containing sequestered iron once or twice to keep the leaves a healthy green colour, and repeat when necessary if the leaves start to look pale.

Make sure the greenhouse is well ven-

Many greenhouse plants, including azaleas, require plenty of humidity in the summer. During particularly dry, sunny weather it is a good idea to damp down the greenhouse path with a hose or watering can. As the water evaporates from the surface of the path, it will keep the atmosphere in the greenhouse humid. This also helps tomatoes, peppers and aubergines to set, and is a deterrent to red spider mite.

Azaleas (*Azalea indica*) are not the easiest plants to grow under glass, but if you are successful you will be rewarded with a glorious show of brightly coloured blooms.

tilated as spring progresses, so the plants do not get too hot. From June until September put the pots outside in the garden. Choose a sheltered and lightly shaded spot where the soil is moist, ideally under trees, and plunge the pots up to their rims into the soil. Keep them lightly watered, occasionally spray with water, and continue feeding as usual. In mid September put them back in the greenhouse, and keep them moist and shaded from direct sun. Spray as before with benomyl if any grey mould appears.

Azaleas prefer a minimum temperature of 10°C (50°F), though they will tolerate 7·5°C (45°F) so long as they are kept slightly drier than usual. If you cannot maintain the latter temperature, it is prob-ably safer to move plants back indoors when the nights start getting cold, around late October. Otherwise, keep them in the greenhouse until most of the buds are showing colour, then move them indoors to flower.

While they are in bud or in flower, keep azaleas moist but not waterlogged, and regularly fed. It is not practical to propagate new plants at home; if you find you can keep them succesfully however, a very cheap way of increasing your stock is to buy plants that have finished flowering after Christmas (often half price or less) and grow them on.

CACTI AND SUCCULENTS
These are fascinating little plants. They are very collectable, and as a result of their popularity there are now countless varieties to choose from. Contrary to popular belief, cacti do not just flower in deserts; nor do they just flower every seven years or only when they are 100 years old – many kinds flower every year, even from an early age.

Display Species of Mammillaria and Rebutia can be relied upon to produce a particularly good show of spring flowers.

Cacti and other succulents can make a fascinating collection for the greenhouse. There are hundreds of varieties to choose from, many of which produce beautiful flowers.

Orchid cacti (*Epiphyllums*) also flower freely each year and have large, spectacular flowers. Some cacti are grown for their weird shapes, such as the prickly pears (*Opuntia*), or for their ferocious spines, such as *Ferocactus*.

Succulents, too, normally flower quite well from early in life; some kinds, like the living stones (*Lithops*), are very small and actually resemble stones. Many, like *Euphorbia*, have strange shapes, or spiky leaves, like *Aloe* and *Agave*.

Cultivation As a general rule, cacti and succulents are desert plants that like plenty of sun, a good gritty compost, and not too much water, especially in winter when most kinds are best kept entirely dry and at a temperature only just above freezing 4°–5°C (38–40°F).

In spring, when plants begin growing naturally, water by spraying once or twice a week. Do not begin watering the soil until plants have quite clearly made some new growth – start watering too early and they may rot.

Repot plants that need it in the spring, again just as they start to grow. Use a proper cactus compost, or mix half grit

with John Innes seed compost. Water sparingly for several weeks.

Feeding and watering Compared to most greenhouse plants, cacti and succulents need very little watering at the best of times – they should be allowed to dry out between waterings, even in summer. If they are overwatered, there is a strong risk that they may rot.

Being slow growing, the plants need

little feeding, perhaps just once or twice a year – in the spring when they start into growth, and again when they are in bud or flower. Special cactus fertilizers are available, and are ideal.

Forest cacti Many kinds of cacti do not grow in deserts, but in trees in the tropical rain forests. These plants, which include orchid cacti, Easter and Christmas cacti, have different cultivation requirements from desert cacti.

During the growing season, feed and water them rather more than normal cacti, and shade them from strong direct sun. They tend to flower better if placed out in the garden for the summer, with their pots plunged up to their rims in moist soil in a sheltered, slightly shaded spot.

Bring them back into the greenhouse in September. Keep the plants much drier in winter, but not completely dry (like normal cacti), watering them just enough to stop the leaves from shrivelling. Rain forest cacti and most succulents need a slightly higher minimum winter temperature than desert cacti – about 4·5°–7·5°C (40°–45°F) is best.

Living stones These plants also require slightly different treatment from other kinds of cacti or succulents. They originate from particularly inhospitable

This Mammillaria produces gorgeous bright red flowers in the spring.

Lithops, or living stones, are among the most unusual plants that can be grown in the greenhouse, with their strange, pebble-like appearance and daisy-like flowers.

deserts where they are only able to grow for a limited part of the year. You must therefore duplicate this short growing season, or the plants will soon die. You must also keep them completely dry until they show signs of starting to grow naturally (which is not normally until quite well into summer), when they may be watered.

The new plant bodies will emerge from the dried up remains of the old ones, flower (if large enough to do so), and within a few weeks start to shrivel again. When this happens, reduce the watering gradually and allow them to dry out when they are ready. Don't try and make the plants keep growing by giving them water when they want to be dry – it doesn't work!

Propagation Cacti and succulents are surprisingly easy to propagate. Those that produce stems, including the Christmas cacti and orchard cacti, can be propagated by cuttings placed in sharp sand; opuntias are propagated by detaching a fully grown young pad and pushing it half way into a pot of sharp sand.

Globular cacti that have rotted off at the base due to overwatering can often be rerooted by slicing the rotten part away, dipping the cut section in hormone rooting powder, and treating it as a cutting. Some plants, such as small clump-forming Mammillarias and Rebutias naturally produce lots of small bodies. With these, individual bodies can be detached from the group and rooted like cuttings.

Many kinds of cacti and succulents, including living stones and mother-in-law's tongue (*Sanseveria*), can be propagated by dividing large old plants or removing well established offsets and potting them separately – the best time to do this is just when growth starts. Many cacti and succulents can also be propagated from seed, though this is a slow and specialist job.

If you get really interested in this group of plants, it pays to join one of the specialist societies; many large towns have a branch holding regular meetings. They will give you the chance to learn more about them – many individual varieties have special demands and you can also swap plants and obtain unusual seeds.

55

Calceolaria, or slipper flowers, are colourful pot plants that can be raised from seed each year as annuals. They are available in a range of yellows, reds and oranges.

Below: Carnivorous plants require humidity and should be protected from bright sunlight. They are fascinating plants to grow, although their unusual requirements make them a little more difficult to accommodate than most other greenhouse plants.

CALCEOLARIA

Pretty annual pot plants which flower in winter and early spring, producing large groups of brightly coloured flowers shaped like segments of an orange. Plants just starting to flower are available in autumn and winter, and will keep flowering for about six weeks in the greenhouse. But it can be fun to raise your own plants from seed.

Sowing and growing Calceolaria are slightly tricky to grow, and need a little care to be successful. The seeds must be sown in mid summer, sprinkled thinly on the surface of the compost, and not covered over; just put a piece of cling film plastic over the top of the pot.

When the seedlings are big enough to handle, prick them out into 9 cm ($3\frac{1}{2}$ in pots). The largest, fastest growing plants can be potted on again, into 13 cm (5 in) pots if you want a few big specimens. Both seedlings and young plants must be kept as cool and shady as possible, and never allowed to dry out. They also need humid air around them all the time. The best way of providing the right conditions is to grow them under the staging in a greenhouse with glass down to the ground, standing them on capillary matting which is kept permanently damp.

Feed and water regularly, and gradually get the plants accustomed to more light as they grow bigger, though they will always need to be shaded from very bright sun. Spray over with water and damp the house down on hot days to maintain high humidity. In the autumn it may be advisable to spray against grey mould, to which the plants are rather prone.

When flower buds are well formed and colourful, plants can be moved into the house if you wish, or left to make a winter display out in the greenhouse. When the flowers are past their best, throw the old plants away because they are annuals and die after flowering.

CAPSICUM

Another popular winter pot plant, grown for its brightly coloured fruit, which resemble miniature peppers in shades of red, purple, orange, green and gold. Plants are available from early autumn onwards and last for two to three months after they start

producing peppers. But you can grow your own from seeds which are sown any time during spring and summer.

Sowing and growing Keep the pots of seed moist and shaded from the sun, and grow the young seedlings on in the same conditions. When they are big enough, pot them individually into 9 cm ($3\frac{1}{2}$ in) pots, and gradually accustom them to more light. They will still need to be kept permanently moist, but not saturated, and shaded from the strongest sun.

Peppers will start forming from autumn onwards, depending on when you sowed the seed. It is best to sow several batches at different dates to give you a succession of plants lasting all winter. Plants may be taken indoors when they are in fruit, or left to make a display in the greenhouse. After fruiting has finished, the plants should be thrown away.

CINERARIA
Most attractive winter and early spring flowering pot plants, with large single daisy-like flowers in a wide range of bright colours. Plants in flower are available

from autumn onwards. They last about four weeks indoors but up to six or seven weeks in the greenhouse where conditions are cooler.

You can also grow your own plants from seed, but like calceolaria they are slightly tricky to grow as the seeds must be sown in the greenhouse in summer, and kept cool, moist and shaded. Sow the seeds and grow the young plants on in the same way as described for calceolaria (see page 56). A June sowing will give you flowering plants at Christmas. You could also make two or three other sowings in May and July for plants to provide a succession of flowers from late autumn through into early spring. Throw the old plants away when they finish flowering, and raise new plants each year.

CARNIVOROUS PLANTS
Carnivorous plants include the well-known sundews, pitcher plants, and Venus fly traps that are popular despite their unusual feeding habits.

They have rather different requirements from most greenhouse plants, and in fact many people set up their green-

Cineraria is a pretty annual that provides attractive flowering pot plants during the winter months.

Like calceolaria, they demand extra care if they are to be successfully raised from seed.

houses specially to grow nothing but carnivorous plants, thus making it easier to provide the conditions they need. However, with care, you can grow them successfully alongside other plants in a mixed collection. It is worth trying one or two plants, as they are fascinating to grow.

Cultivation In general, carnivorous plants need humid conditions and slight shade – enough to protect them from bright sunlight. They need constant moisture in summer, when their pots should be stood in a trough containing 2·5–5 cm (1–2 in) of soft water (either rain water, or water that has been boiled in the kettle and cooled). Just as important, they should never be fed with normal plant food – instead they must always be allowed to catch insects, which they digest and use as their source of nutrients.

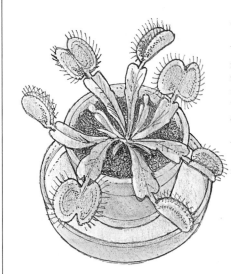

GROWING CARNIVOROUS PLANTS
To help carnivorous plants thrive in summer, stand them in a trough or saucer containing 3–5 cm (1¼–2 in) of soft water – either rain water or water that has been boiled and allowed to cool. Keep the plants humid and shaded, but never feed them with plant fertilizers of any kind. If their natural food (flies) is in short supply, you can attract more by hanging a small piece of meat nearby.

important that a minimum temperature of 4·5°C (40°F) be maintained.

Growth and propagation Carnivorous plants are not the easiest of species to cultivate; nor do they grow very fast – in fact they will be perfectly happy in their original pots for one or two years.

When repotting is necessary it is best to buy the special compost for carnivorous plants; normal potting compost will not do.

These plants are not the easiest to propagate; they do not make the sort of growth that allows cuttings to be taken, and all except the sundews are slow and difficult to raise from seed.

Established plants can be divided up when they have grown into large clumps. Sundews may occasionally seed themselves into other pots, and these seedlings can be potted individually. Again, if you take a real fancy to this group of plants, it is a good idea to join the Carnivorous Plant Society for both information and supplies of seeds.

Dionaea muscipula, the Venus fly trap, is the most popular of all the carnivorous plants. It does not require very deep compost and is quite happy grouped with others in a shallow pan.

From October to early April the plants should be kept rather drier; take them out of the watering trough and just hand water occasionally when the compost becomes very dry. During this time it is

CHRYSANTHEMUMS

Chrysanthemums are a large group of plants which are categorized primarily according to when they flower. Early varieties flower in late summer or early autumn, and are planted outdoors in the garden. Later flowering chrysanthemums bloom after the frosts have started, so they are grown in pots which are stood outdoors in summer and brought into the greenhouse in September to protect the flowers from frost. They generally flower in November or December. New chrysanthemum plants are grown each year from cuttings and it is possible to buy them already rooted.

Propagation If you have grown chrysanthemums before, the old plants can be kept and used to take cuttings. To do this, cut the old plants back to several centimetres above the ground after flowering, and store them in a frost-free place overwinter. They should be potted up in peat in January or February, and kept in a warm place – such as a propagator – to force them into growth.

When shoots start to appear, take them as cuttings when they are 10 cm (4 in) long. Chrysanthemum cuttings root easily in pots of seed compost or sharp sand in the propagator, in temperatures of 16–18·5°C (60–65°F).

Cultivation Whether you root your own cuttings or buy them, pot them up into 9 cm ($3\frac{1}{2}$ in) pots and grow on in a frost-free greenhouse. Water them sparingly to start with, giving the young plants just enough water to prevent them from wilting until they are established.

It is also usual to stop chrysanthemum cuttings once or twice before they are more than several centimetres high, making them produce more shoots and an abundance of flowers.

When they begin growing strongly, increase the watering and start feeding

Above right: Chrysanthemums can provide a plentiful supply of long-lasting cut flowers for the home.

Below right: 'Autumn Days' is an intermediate type: the petals are partly 'incurved' and partly 'reflexed'.

regularly with a general-purpose liquid feed. Pot the greenhouse flowering varieties into 13 cm (5 in) pots once the roots start growing out through the drainage hole in the bottom of the original containers.

Hardening off Two weeks before chrysanthemums for the garden are planted out, they should be hardened off – stand their pots outdoors during the day, but bring them in at night. This should be done during a warm spell in April or May.

Winter flowering greenhouse chrysanthemums should be similarly hardened off and moved outside at the same time. Pot them on into 20–25 cm (8–10 in) sized pots when they outgrow the 13 cm (5 in) sized ones.

Support and training Both types of chrysanthemums will need to be supported to keep their stems straight – push one or more 13 cm (5 in) canes in beside each plant and tie the stems loosely to it with soft string or raffia. When the first tiny flower buds appear at the tops of the stems, decide whether you want 'spray' chrysanthemums (which have several small flowers on each stem) or 'bloom' (which have one very large flower per stem).

To grow sprays, nip out the crown bud (the large one at the very tip of the shoot), leaving the cluster of smaller buds behind. If you want large single blooms, remove all the small buds from the stem and leave only the large crown bud. Do this disbudding while the buds are still very small.

Autumn Towards the end of September move the pots of winter flowering chrysanthemums back into the greenhouse. The house should be heated just enough to keep it frost-free, and ventilated well at every opportunity to avoid grey mould, which can spoil the developing flowers. If it does become troublesome, rather than spray, use smoke cones to control grey mould. These are similar to fireworks – you just light the touchpaper,

SPRAY AND BLOOM CHRYSANTHEMUMS
1. To produce spray chrysanthemums, with lots of small blooms on each stem, pinch out the larger 'crown' bud when the buds are still very small.

2. To produce bloom chrysanthemums, with a single, large flower on each stem, pinch out all the side buds, leaving just the crown bud to develop.

The spray chrysanthemums make beautiful pot plants for the home, with masses of long-lasting blooms on each plant.

Another popular subject for flowering pot plants, cyclamen can be raised in a shady part of a heated greenhouse and will last longer there than plants grown indoors. A few named varieties are obtainable and there is a range of white, pink and red shades from which to choose.

and then shut the greenhouse door, and watch it fill with fungicide smoke.

Cut flowers Cut both indoor and outdoor chrysanthemums when the flowers are just fully open. Provided they are put straight into clean water, the cut flowers can last from four to six weeks indoors. When all the flowers have been cut, prune back the old stems and either dig up the roots or allow the pots to dry out, keeping them for cuttings the following spring.

CYCLAMEN
Popular flowering pot plants for winter and early spring decoration. Cyclamen plants are sold in flower throughout the autumn and winter. Although they are usually grown indoors, they also make ideal plants for a heated greenhouse as the flowers will last longer there. Do not raise them indoors – it can be too warm.

Cultivation Under glass, cyclamen like a minimum winter temperature of 4·5°C (40°F). While they are growing and flowering, they need to be kept just moist, and occasionally fed with a well-diluted liquid feed. They must also be shaded from direct sun.

By late March the plants will be starting to decline – no new flowers will be produced and the leaves turn yellow. This is quite natural, and indicates that the plants are preparing to become dormant. When this happens, gradually reduce the watering and stop feeding the plants. The leaves will soon dry out and fall off, leaving just the dormant corm. The pots can be tipped on their sides and stored under the greenhouse staging for the summer. During this time they should be kept perfectly dry. (Putting them on their sides prevents water dripping into the pots which make the corms rot.)

New growth Around the beginning of August cyclamen will start growing again. When the first new leaves appear, stand the pots upright and put them back on the staging, keeping them heavily shaded. (In a glass-to-ground greenhouse, grow them in the shade under the staging.) Begin watering, a little at first, and delay feeding till the first flower buds appear. Feed occasionally from then on. Plants can be taken indoors temporarily while they are looking their best, or left in the greenhouse to make a winter display. The same corms can be re-used for several years,

though the best flowers are generally produced on younger plants.

Seedlings New plants are grown from seed which can be sown any time in spring or summer. Keep the young seedlings permanently just moist, and well shaded from the sun. Pot them individually into 9 cm (3½ in) pots when they are big enough, leaving the top half of the corm above the level of the compost. Repot them into 13 cm (5 in) pots when they outgrow the original containers, after which the plants will not need further repotting. From the time you sow seeds, it takes about 18 months to have young cyclamen ready to start flowering.

FREESIAS
Freesias make interesting, if slightly untidy, plants to grow in a greenhouse, which must be heated to 4·5°C (40°F) in winter. The flowers, which are brightly coloured and highly scented, are produced in spring. They make a good display under glass if left on the plants, but are normally used as cut flowers indoors.

Cultivation Freesia corms are available in the autumn. Make sure you buy

Cyclamen add a beautiful splash of winter colour in the heated greenhouse among other tender subjects – here they are displayed with some Agave and Smithiantha.

those for greenhouse cultivation and not the kind intended for growing out in the garden. Plant the corms as soon as they arrive. Put six in around the sides of a 13 cm (5 in) pot filled with potting compost, so the tips are just below the surface of the compost. Water them in lightly, and do not water again until the foliage starts to grow. From then on, water freesias sparingly at all times.

Meanwhile push a few split canes in round the sides of the pot, and crisscross between them with soft string. This supports both foliage and flower stems, keeps the plants from sprawling too badly, and is also essential for keeping the flower stalks straight. If you want particularly straight stems, tie each flower spike individually to its own split cane.

Flowering and dormancy From the time the flower spikes start to appear,

reduce watering to the bare minimum. Flowers may be cut when each stem has one flower fully open, and most of the remaining buds showing their true colour. They last well in water when cut fresh. After the flowers have either been cut or there are no more on the plant, resume watering normally and give regular liquid feeds, building up the corms for next year's display.

When the foliage starts to yellow, the bulbs are preparing to become dormant for the summer and watering should gradually be reduced until the old leaves die and fall off. When the corms are completely dormant and dry, knock them out of their pots and keep them in a cool, dark place before replanting again in the early autumn.

Propagation Freesia plants propagate themselves – your original six corms will most likely have increased themselves to twelve, or more, by the end of their first season's growth. When you replant them, it is a good idea to put the largest corms together in the same pot, since this is the way in which they will flower best. Small

corms may not flower in their first year, needing to reach a good size first.

Freesias can also be grown from seeds, which are sown in the greenhouse in spring. Keep the seedlings well shaded from the sun, and constantly just moist – but not too wet. Feed them regularly throughout the summer, and keep them growing through winter. Some of the stronger seedlings may flower in their first year. Allow the plants to go dormant when the leaves yellow in late spring, and expect most of them to start flowering during the following year.

GERBERA
Gerberas are brightly coloured South African daisies that are very popular as cut flowers, and can be grown without much difficulty in the greenhouse border. The plants form a rosette of grey-green leaves shaped rather like those of a dandelion, from the centre of which the flowers grow on long stalks.

Varieties Since plants are rarely available it is best to grow your own from seed. Choose *Gerbera jamesonii*, or one of the

Above and right: With their brightly coloured, highly scented flowers, freesias make a beautiful display in the greenhouse and are among the longest lasting of all cut flowers.
Below: Dwarf gerberas are available as pot plants, but you can also grow your own from seed.

tall stemmed hybrids. Dwarf gerberas are an innovation, and are often sold as pot plants, though they too can be grown from seed. Varieties such as 'Dwarf Frisbee' or 'Happipot' are suitable.

Cultivation Sow seed of gerbera in February in a heated propagator at 18·5°C (65°F) if possible, otherwise delay sowing until late April or May when the weather is warmer. (Late sown plants may not flower in their first year.) Prick the seedlings out when they are big enough, and then pot them into 9 cm ($3\frac{1}{2}$ in) pots. Dwarf varieties should be potted on into 13 cm (5 in) half pots. Full-sized types are best planted out into the border – 30–45 cm (12–18in) apart – when their original pots are filled with roots.

Gerberas need a warm sunny situation and dislike too much humidity. Water the plants sparingly, and feed regularly with a general-purpose liquid or soluble feed. Pot plants can be taken indoors when they come into flower, or left in the greenhouse for decoration.

Flowers of tall-stemmed varieties can be gathered as soon as they are fully open. Do not cut them in the usual way, instead pull the stems as you would rhubarb, taking care not to pull up the plant at the same time. In winter, keep gerberas almost dry, and cut off any dead leaves. If they are kept very dry they will survive in a greenhouse kept barely frost-free, but plants get through the winter in better condition if you maintain a minimum winter temperature of 4·5°C (40°F).

LEMONS
Though growing lemon trees from pips is an interesting exercise, it is unlikely the trees will ever produce any fruit. Buying a grafted plant is a much better bet. This way, you will get lots of full-sized edible fruit from a plant of a manageable size, even in the first year. The flowers are delightful too – not only are they beautifully scented, but they are produced almost continuously. It is common to find flowers, and both green and ripe lemons, on the same plant virtually all the year round. This prolific nature, coupled with attractive camellia-like evergreen leaves, makes lemons amongst the most attractive of greenhouse plants to grow. They are surprisingly easy too.

Named varieties are occasionally available. 'Meyers Lemon' is probably the best to grow as it produces a reliable crop of large fruit, and only needs a minimum temperature of 4·5°C (40°F) in winter, whereas most other citrus plants need from 7·5–10°C (45–50°F).

Cultivation Repot lemon plants every spring into a larger sized pot and John Innes potting compost No. 3, until eventually they end up in 30–38 cm (12–15 in) pots. In subsequent years, top dress instead, replacing the top layer of compost with fresh John Innes compost No. 3.

Feed and water well during the growing season, but in winter keep the compost much drier. However, an occasional light watering will be needed to stop the leaves from shrivelling or falling off.

Pruning and pests Plants will need pruning in the autumn or spring to keep them in shape and prevent them from getting too big. Cut out entirely any branches that are dead or damaged, and shorten back any that are too long by half or one third their length. Always cut just above a leaf joint.

When the fruit appears, do not be in too much of a hurry to pick it. Let the fruit remain on the plants until fully ripe, when they will be coloured deep yellow, and taste much better than shop-bought lemons that are often picked when they are still bright green.

Lemon plants are not affected much by pests, such as greenfly, as their leaves are too tough for the insects to feed on. However, they are often attacked by scale insect, so look under the leaves regularly and spray as soon as any appear. If left unchecked the plant can be badly damaged, and the leaves will also be covered with black sooty mould.

It is not practical to propagate new lemon trees at home, as they have to be grafted. However, the original plant will be long lived if well looked after, and can be expected to produce a few lemons at a time almost all the year round.

PASSION FLOWER
Climbing perennial pot plants best known for their extraordinary flowers, although many of the less well known varieties also produce edible passion fruit, just like those found in supermarkets.

Left: The passion flower that is most commonly available as a pot plant, *Passiflora caerulea*. Like other passion flowers, it can be trained up canes or wire netting to develop into a large and decorative climber in the greenhouse.

Opposite: *Passiflora quadrangularis* is one of the varieties of passion flower grown for its edible fruits.

Although poinsettias are a familiar sight at Christmas, they naturally produce their red bracts in the spring. If you propagate your own plants from cuttings expect them to flower around Easter.

open at the same time for this to happen – they are not self-fertile). They are ready to eat some time after they have turned purple, when the skin wrinkles. The fruit will easily fall from the plant when it is ripe. Passion fruit are eaten rather like boiled eggs; just slice the top off and eat the contents with a spoon. Fruit are produced a few at a time throughout mid and late summer.

The plants will start shedding their leaves towards autumn. When this happens, gradually cut down the watering to prepare them for their winter rest. Once all the leaves have fallen, cut the old stems down to 15 cm (6 in) from the base of the plant, and remove all the dead leaves which could otherwise go mouldy. Keep the plants fairly dry in winter, though an occasional light watering may be needed to stop the remaining stems from shrivelling. When new shoots start to appear in spring, gradually begin watering again.

Plants can be grown from seed sown in the spring (these won't fruit until they are two to three years old). They can also be grown from cuttings taken in spring or summer, though they are not as easy to root as many greenhouse plants.

POINSETTIA

Poinsettias are popular, traditional Christmas pot plants, with bright red, pink or white bracts (the true flowers are the tiny yellow elements in the centre). The plants are not suited for growing permanently in the greenhouse as they need higher winter temperatures than would be economical. However, it is useful to keep plants in the greenhouse after they have finished flowering, when they have lost their looks. Poinsettias are not the easiest of plants to keep, and many people find it easier just to throw away the old plants and buy new ones each year. If you want to try keeping them, this is what to do.

Plants of the common passion flower (*Passiflora caerulea*) are readily available. This species is grown for its flowers, and rarely produces fruit, which would be egg-shaped, yellow, and not suitable for eating. If you do want fruits, grow *P. edulis* or *P. quadrangularis*. Both have large and fascinating flowers, followed by egg-sized fruit which start off green and slowly turn purple as they ripen. These plants are occasionally available, otherwise you will have to grow your own from seed.

Cultivation Passion flowers are easy plants to grow. They thrive best in a warm sunny spot. Grow them in large pots and train the stems up a framework of canes, or alternatively plant them in the border and let the stems ramble up wire netting on the side of the greenhouse. It is important to water and feed the plants well during the growing season.

The fruit start to swell almost as soon as the flowers are over, provided they have been pollinated (you need two flowers

Cultivation When the flowers are over, take the plants out to the greenhouse and cut the stems down to about 10 cm (4 in) above the top of the pot. Dab a little sharp sand on to the cut to stop the white sap bleeding out (wash your hands afterwards as the sap is an irritant). Repot if necessary, and water very sparingly until the plant starts making new growth. Then increase the watering, but always keep poinsettias rather drier than normal greenhouse plants. Feed them occasionally. Grow poinsettias shaded from the very brightest sun during the summer.

In the autumn, when the weather starts getting cold, it is advisable to move the plants back into the greenhouse as they need a minimum temperature of 13°C (55°F). Do not be surprised if they do not produce new red bracts for Christmas – they are specially treated at the nursery to make them flower out of season. They will probably flower again around Easter.

Primulas are available in hundreds of different colours and can be grown from seed for winter and spring flowering.

Propagation   Poinsettias can be propagated by cuttings. It is most convenient to use the stems you cut off in late spring for cuttings, though you can take them from plants any time during the spring and summer. They root best in sharp sand.

Plants you raise yourself from cuttings will grow much bigger than those you have bought. This is because the bought plants will have been treated with a chemical dwarfing agent that is not available to amateur growers. However, plants can be stopped once or twice to give them a bushier appearance.

PRIMULA

Several different kinds of primula are grown as winter and early spring flowering pot plants – *Primula obconica,*

P. malacoides, P. sinensis, and several good hybrids. You can buy the plants when they are in flower but for a wider choice of unusual kinds it is best to grow your own from seeds.

Propagation   To have flowers for Christmas, sow *P. obconica* at the end of January, *P. sinensis* in March, and *P. malacoides* in April. If you want more plants to flower later in the spring, make another sowing of each of these a few weeks after the first.

Cultivation   Greenhouse primulas need to be grown in permanent shade and moisture. Sow the seeds on the surface of the compost (don't cover it), and stand the pots in a shallow tray of water to keep

Above: *Primula obconica* is one of the most popular varieties for growing under glass, with colours ranging from white, pink and red to lilac, mauve and even blue.

Right: Although Streptocarpus, or Cape primrose, are often sold as pot plants for indoor display, they are easier to cultivate in a heated greenhouse, since they require a constantly humid atmosphere.

2. Fill a 5 cm (2 in) pot with general purpose compost and, using a small stick or the end of a pencil, make a hole 4 cm (1½ in) deep in the centre. Push the cut end of the leaf in and firm well. Water in well and keep constantly humid until the cutting is well rooted and a new plant has started to grow.

TAKING STREPTOCARPUS LEAF CUTTINGS
1. Cut a young but full size leaf from near the centre of an established plant. Use a sharp knife and cut the leaf as near to its base as possible.

3. Sometimes you will find more than one plant growing from a single cutting. When the plants are big enough to handle, pot each one individually. The leaf can be removed once the plants are growing well.

them damp. Seed can go into the propagator to germinate but it is not essential – what is vital is that the pots are kept shaded, and at a temperature below 16°C (60°F) or they will not be able to germinate until the temperature drops.

When the seedlings are big enough, prick them out into trays and then pot them into 9 cm (3½ in) pots. Use peat-based compost, and again keep the plants permanently moist and well shaded. In an all-glass greenhouse, the best place to grow them is on moist capillary matting underneath the staging.

Display Feed regularly, and when the flower stems appear take extra care the plants do not dry out at all. Plants in full flower can be taken indoors, or left in the greenhouse for winter display. After

flowering, primula plants are thrown away and new plants are raised from seed each year.

STREPTOCARPUS
Cape primrose, or Streptocarpus, are pretty little plants with long strap-like leaves and large exotic looking flowers in a wide range of colours. They are much easier to grow in a slightly heated greenhouse than they are indoors, as the plants like a constantly humid atmosphere. They must also be kept well shaded from direct sun, and will grow particularly well under the staging of an all-glass greenhouse.

Cultivation Plants should be kept just moist during the growing season – spring to late summer – and fed regularly, especially when in flower. Old leaves which have

become broken or damaged should be cut off, as should dead flower stems, to keep plants looking their best.

Propagation Streptocarpus can be propagated from seed in spring or from leaf cuttings taken in spring or late summer. They are not the easiest plants to propagate successfully, because the seedlings or cuttings must never be allowed to dry out. It helps to stand the pots on damp capillary matting to maintain the necessary moisture.

Young plants are very slow growing at first, and will probably only flower towards the end of their first year. Old plants can be split up in spring or autumn; plants produced this way are much easier to manage and also have the advantage of flowering sooner.

A NURSERY FOR PLANTS AND VEGETABLES

Although tomatoes, peppers, aubergines, cucumbers, melons and many bedding plants and annuals can be raised on windowsills indoors, much better results will be obtained in the more controlled environment of a greenhouse.

TOMATOES, PEPPERS AND AUBERGINES

If you want to raise your own tomato, pepper and aubergine plants, a heated greenhouse is almost essential. The plants are initially slow growing, and need to be sown early in spring and kept in high temperatures, otherwise they will not start cropping until very late in the summer. It is sometimes possible to raise reasonable plants by sowing seed on a warm, well-lit indoor windowsill, but results are not so reliable. Unless you have the proper facilities, it is normally better to buy plants when you are ready to plant them.

SOWING AND PRICKING OUT

To raise greenhouse tomato, pepper and aubergine plants, sow the seeds thinly in pots in a temperature of 16°–21°C (60°–70°F) during February or early March. (An electrically heated, thermostatically controlled propagator is the most economical way of providing the temperature needed.) Keep the seed compost just moist but take care not to overwater as damping off is always a problem with early sowings. (Water with cheshunt compound or spray with liquid copper if damping off is a problem.)

When the seedlings have come through, wait until the first pair of leaves (seed leaves) have opened out fully before pricking them out. Handle the seedlings by their leaves, not by the stems. Prick out only the strongest seedlings, as you will probably only need a few plants, but do prick out half a dozen or so more seedlings than you need plants. This allows you to choose the pick of the bunch at planting time.

Put the seedlings into clean trays, filled with a good peat-based seed compost. When pricking out, plant the seedlings right up to their necks in the compost, so the seed leaves are almost resting on the surface. Do this even if the seedlings have become a little drawn up and leggy, as it produces better plants.

Return the pots of young seedlings to the propagator after watering them in, and grow them on at the same temperature, 16–21°C (60–70°F), for another few weeks.

GENERAL CARE OF YOUNG PLANTS

Ventilate the propagator slightly on fine days (most kinds have vents in the lid), to prevent fungal disease, but shut the vents

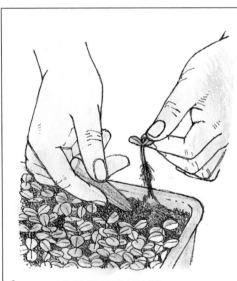

PRICKING OUT SEEDLINGS
1. Prick out the seedlings, when the seed leaves have just opened out and they are large enough to handle. It helps if you loosen the roots gently with a plant tag.

2. Plant them in rows in another tray of fresh compost. Make small holes with a plant tag, setting the seedlings so their leaves are just above the surface of the compost.

3. After filling the tray with seedlings, water them in lightly, before returning them to the propagator for another few weeks.

again at night. Then start acclimatizing the young plants to cooler conditions very slowly.

Start when the young plants are several centimetres high, gradually reducing the temperature in the propagator to 10°C (50°F) when the plants are 10–13 cm (4–5 in) high. Then start hardening the plants off, by removing the lid of the propagator during the day, and replacing it at night. After a week or so, the plants should be ready to leave the propagator and take their place on the greenhouse staging. Keep the heating in the green-

house set as high as you can, ideally at 10°C (50°F), but certainly no lower than 7·5°C (45°F).

During the entire propagation period keep a close watch on the plants and spray them as soon as you see the first signs of any fungal disease – some growers like to spray this group of plants fortnightly with benomyl as a precaution. Although the disease is normally the main problem, keep a watch out for greenfly or whitefly, too, and again spray if necessary.

Water the plants sparingly so as not to encourage over-lush growth, but when

Tomatoes, such as 'Gardener's Delight' can be raised from seed and then grown outdoors if you have a heated greenhouse. Sow in early spring, to ensure ripening before the end of the summer.

you do water – ideally once a week – give them a diluted liquid tomato feed made up to the usual strength. When the young plants fill their pots with roots, they are ready for planting.

By this time the tomato plants should have their first flowers just opening – if not, delay planting for a while as tomatoes tend to grow rather too leafy unless they are planted in flower. Do not wait for peppers and aubergines to flower, but plant as soon as the roots start coming out through the bottom of the pot. If you wait too long, they suffer a check in growth from which they never really recover, and the inevitable result is that cropping will also be jeopardized.

CUCUMBERS AND MELONS

Cucumber and melon plants do not need sowing as early as tomatoes, since they are much faster growing plants.

SOWING

If you have a cold greenhouse you can raise your own cucumber or melon plants by sowing them during May, or even as late as June. Or you can raise them on a warm indoor windowsill, sowing in late April or early May. If you have a heated greenhouse and propagator, though, sow the seeds in mid March at a temperature of 21°C (70°F).

To raise cucumber and melon plants, sow the seeds singly in 9 cm ($3\frac{1}{2}$ in) pots, half filled with a good peat-based seed compost. They germinate very quickly.

GENERAL CARE

When the seed leaves open out, start to top up the pots with more seed compost, 13 mm ($\frac{1}{2}$ in) at a time. This has the same effect as pricking out seedlings up to their necks. This individual treatment avoids any damage to either the plants or their roots, and is advisable since cucumbers and melon plants are rather sensitive in their early stages.

Start gradually lowering the temperature in the propagator a few degrees at a time, until by the time the plants have three or four leaves the temperature is down to 10°C (50°F). The plants will need a little more watering than tomato plants. After three to four weeks, start to give them a well diluted feed once or twice a week using a general-purpose liquid or soluble feed.

Spray with fungicide if necessary, but cucumber plants are notorious for dying off very quickly if anything goes wrong with them, and it is easier to raise new plants than try and save sick ones. Harden

the plants off as described for tomatoes, and plant them out as soon as the roots start to show through the holes in the bottom of the pot. As with peppers and aubergines, plants will not grow so successfully if they are allowed to become pot bound, so check to make sure that this does not happen.

BEDDING PLANTS

Annual bedding plants come in two basic types; hardy annuals and half-hardy annuals (HA or HHA). Hardy annuals include sweet peas, cornflowers, larkspur, pot marigolds (*Calendula*), alyssum,

Sweet pea seedlings in trays of seed compost. When they fill the tray, it's time to harden them off. Stand outside during the day, and bring them in at night, before planting outdoors permanently.

godetia, sunflowers, nasturtiums and love-in-a-mist (*Nigella*). Examples of half-hardy annuals are anthirrinums, bedding dahlias, morning glory (*Ipomoea*), salvia, French and African marigolds (*Tagetes*), tobacco plants (*Nicotiana*), lobelia, petunias and zinnias. Seed packets are always marked to show which are hardy and which half-hardy—an important

Above: Half-hardy annual seeds can only be successfully raised in a heated greenhouse. When the seed leaves have formed, making the seedlings large enough to handle, it's time to prick them out.

Being hardy annuals, nasturtium seeds can be usually sown outdoors. On wet, heavy soil, or during a cold spring, however, it's advisable to raise them in a greenhouse, and then plant out later.

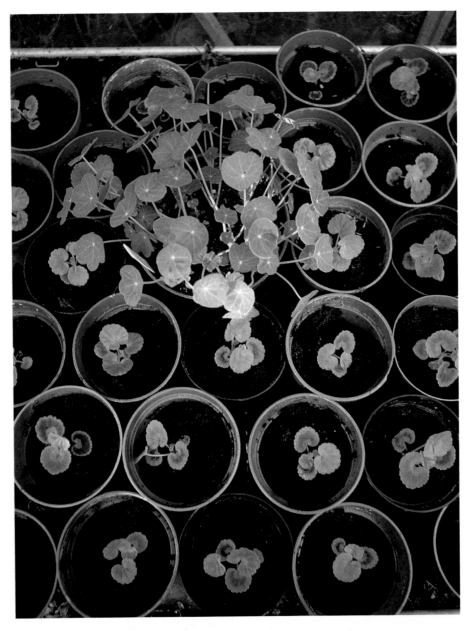

to overwater whilst not letting the compost become completely dry either. Watch out for seedlings keeling over suddenly, which may indicate damping off. Remove affected seedlings immediately if it occurs, and spray the remainder with cheshunt compound or liquid copper.

Pricking out and growing on When the seedlings are big enough to handle, prick them out into trays of seed compost, spacing them 5 cm (2 in) apart. Handle them by the leaves, not the stems, to avoid bruising. Water them in, and water again whenever the compost starts to feel dryish; there is no need to feed for about four to six weeks after pricking out the seedlings. After that, water with liquid or soluble feed regularly, according to the manufacturer's instructions.

When the plants fill the tray, harden them off for a week or two by standing them outside during the day and bringing them back into the greenhouse at night. Then they are ready to plant out. You do not need to wait until after the risk of frost is over to plant out hardy annuals, though obviously it pays to choose good weather.

HALF-HARDY ANNUALS
Half-hardy annuals need more warmth, and can only be propagated 100 per cent successfully in a heated greenhouse. An electrically heated propagator is a great help, as this is an economical way to provide the high temperatures they need early in life.

Sowing Sow the seed in the same way as for hardy annuals, but after watering them in, place the pots inside the propagator with the thermostat set at 18·5–21°C (65°–70°F).

Cover the lid of the propagator with a piece of old net curtain, or something similar, to shade the seedlings from the sun. Check them every day and when a good number of seedlings are through, gradually start lowering the temperature in the propagator a few degrees at a time.

Pricking out and growing on When the seedlings are big enough, prick them out into trays and then return the trays to the propagator for a week or two longer while you continue lowering the temperature slowly. By the time the seedlings are

distinction as the two are grown in slightly different ways.

What both types have in common is that they must be sown early in spring, during March, or they will not be big enough to start flowering at the beginning of the summer.

HARDY ANNUALS
Hardy annuals do not mind the cold, and can be sown straight into the garden where they are to flower, provided growing conditions are good. But in a cold spring, on wet heavy soil, or if your garden soil is likely to be full of weed seeds which will quickly grow and smother

Zonal geraniums, distinguished by their green leaves with conspicuous darker markings, can be grown from seed (other types of geraniums are usually raised from cuttings).

young seedlings, it is best to grow hardy annuals in trays in the greenhouse, and plant them out later. So long as you only grow hardy annuals, you can raise bedding plants in an unheated greenhouse.

Sowing To raise hardy annuals under glass, sow the seeds in small pots of seed compost, and water them in. Keep them shaded from direct sun, and take care not

almost touching each other you should have hardened them off enough to stand them on the greenhouse staging, where the temperature will only be 4·5°–7·5°C (40°–45°F) at night.

From now on, grow them in exactly the same way as hardy annuals, but taking particular care to harden them off very thoroughly before planting them out. As they dislike cold weather, do not plant half-hardy annuals out until after the date of the last frost expected in your area – this is normally mid May in the south of the country, and early June in the north.

Growing on the windowsill If you do not have a propagator, it is possible to germinate half-hardy annual seeds on a warm indoor windowsill. This needs to be out of direct sunlight, but in good indirect light, or the seedlings will become 'leggy', making them particularly susceptible to fungal diseases.

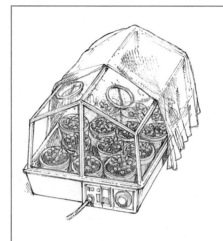

An electrically heated propagator with thermostatic control is ideal for propagating half-hardy annuals. On sunny days, shade the seedlings with fine netting to prevent scorching.

Sow the seeds as described before (see *Sowing*), but after watering them in, stand the pots inside large plastic bags to retain humidity until the seeds have germinated. When the seedlings come through, prick them out into trays – you can buy special kinds for use on windowsills, which have drip trays underneath and plastic covers on top. Once the weather is warm enough, move the trays out to the greenhouse with the heating set at a minimum of 7·5°C (45°F), and grow on as before.

GROWING LATE PLANTS TO FILL GAPS
People sometimes deliberately sow a few bedding plants later, in May or even early June, to produce plants for filling odd gaps that sometimes appear in a border towards the end of the summer.

Mesembry-anthemums are half-hardy annuals suitable for growing in sunny rockeries and on banks.

If you want to do this, sow a few seeds thinly straight into 9 cm ($3\frac{1}{2}$ in) pots on the greenhouse staging, keep them shaded from strong sun, and do not prick them out. Instead, let the plants grow in a clump, and when they fill the pot with roots, transplant the entire group without splitting it up, to wherever more plants are needed in a border.

HERBACEOUS AND BIENNIAL FLOWERS

Herbaceous plants are border plants such as delphinium, lupin and shasta daisy, that die down in winter and come up again every spring. Biennial flowers include wallflowers, sweet Williams and fox-gloves that grow leaves in their first year, flower in their second and are then re-placed with new plants. Both types of plants are commonly grown from seed, which is sown in mid summer, though many perennials can also be grown from cuttings taken in spring. It takes about 6 months to 1 year to have plants ready to go out in the garden. The plants are propagated in spring or summer, planted out in autumn or spring, and flower the year after.

GROWING FROM SEED

You do not need a heated greenhouse or a propagator for growing perennial and biennial flowers from seed, as they are sown in mid summer.

For high quality biennials, like these sweet William, sow seed under glass in summer, keep in a cold greenhouse over winter and plant out the following spring for a summer display.

Sow the seed thinly in pots in the greenhouse, following the same method as for hardy annual bedding plants. Because they are sown during the hottest part of the year, it is most important to keep the pots moist, shaded and as cool as possible all the time. When the seedlings are big enough, prick them out into trays and later pot them into 9 cm ($3\frac{1}{2}$ in) pots. They can then be placed outside for the summer, and the plants set out in their final garden positions in the autumn.

If you want really good quality plants,

TAKING CHRYSANTHEMUM CUTTINGS

1. In early spring, cut shoots growing from chrysanthemum stools just below leaf joints.

2. Remove the lower leaves of the shoot, using a sharp knife, and then push into pots or trays of compost.

3. Place the pots or trays of cuttings in a propagator. They should root quickly if kept at a temperature of 16°C (60°F).

however, it is a good idea to keep them in the greenhouse for the winter (either a cold or frost-free greenhouse is fine). The plants are then planted out in spring, around late March, during a spell of reasonably good weather. This is a particularly useful technique if you garden on wet heavy soil, for young plants that are put out in autumn often rot. They will certainly get off to a better start planted in the spring, unless the soil is excessively free draining. All perennial and biennial plants can be overwintered under glass in pots, except those that flower early in the spring, such as wallflowers. These are best planted in the autumn.

GROWING FROM CUTTINGS

Many kinds of border plants can also be grown from cuttings. This is a useful way of propagating plants you already have growing well in the garden or where you can get cuttings from friends. These cuttings are best taken in early spring, when the first new shoots appear. You need a heated greenhouse, and ideally a heated propagator to guarantee success.

Dahlia and chrysanthemum cuttings are very easy to raise. Both plants are dug up from the garden in autumn and stored in a frost-free place over winter, so the bare roots can be forced to produce the cuttings you need.

Pot the roots in moist peat, and then put in a warm place such as the propagator. When they have grown a few shoots 10 cm (4 in) long, cut them off and use them as cuttings. These will root quickly in the propagator at 16°C (60°F). Old dahlia tubers can be replanted, but old chrysanthemum plants are normally thrown away after producing a good crop of cuttings.

Garden plants such as delphiniums and lupins produce shoots in the garden in early spring and these too can be used as cuttings. Growing such plants from cuttings is a good idea if you want a lot of them and don't mind waiting a year. If you only need one or two new plants, or want immediate results, it is better to dig up and split the old roots in autumn or early spring, giving an immediate supply of new flowering size plants. To take cuttings from these plants, there is no need to dig up the roots and force them. Just cut off a few shoots as soon as they are about

Cuttings are easy to grow from lupin and other herbaceous plants in early spring. When shoots are about 10 cm (4 in) long, cut them away from the stem of a plant just below a joint. For best results, grow the cuttings in a propagator in the greenhouse. Make a hole in the compost with a dibber or wooden stick and insert each cutting firmly. Grow the cuttings in a moist atmosphere at about 16°C (60°F). The roots should develop in about three to four weeks.

77

10 cm (4 in) long and root them as before. (Do not take more than about one third of the shoots from any plant or you will prevent it growing healthily.)

Pot the cuttings when they are well rooted and grow them on until the plants are large enough to plant out in the garden, which will probably be in the autumn. Again, if growing conditions are not very good or you want especially good plants, you could pot them into bigger pots and keep them in a cold or frost-free greenhouse over the winter.

VEGETABLES

Many people sow their vegetable crops straight into the vegetable garden in rows. But if you have a greenhouse, it is worthwhile raising some – or all – of your vegetable plants under cover. Given protection from the weather you can get early crops off to an even earlier start than usual, as well as producing top quality young plants that will give bigger or better crops. A cold greenhouse is all you need for raising most vegetables, but a little heat is useful for producing extra early plants.

Vegetable plants can be divided into two main types, in much the same way as bedding plants. There are the hardy types, cabbages, leeks, etc, which don't mind the cold and can be planted out before the last expected frost, and half-hardy kinds, such as sweet corn, French beans, marrows and courgettes, which cannot be planted out until after the last frost. Like bedding plants, it is important to sow most kinds of vegetables at just the right time if they are to crop properly. With fast growing kinds, like lettuce, though, sowing dates are less precise. These crops can be sown little and often, producing a succession of crops. Full details of the sowing times for individual varieties of vegetables will be found in the instructions on the backs of the seed packets, but the following chart gives a general guide.

Although you can sow lettuce straight into the garden, the results will be better if the seedlings are raised in the greenhouse. Sow seeds every two or three weeks for a steady supply.

VEGETABLE SOWING UNDER GLASS

Crop	Sow	Notes
Broad beans	Feb–Mar	
Broccoli – sprouting	April	
Brussels sprouts	Feb	early varieties
	Mar–April	late varieties
Cabbage – spring	July–Aug	
Cabbage – summer	Feb–Mar	
Cabbage – winter	April–May	
Calabrese	Mar–May	
Cauliflower	Jan–Mar	
Courgettes	April	
Cucumbers – outdoor	April	
French beans	April	
Herbs	Feb–April	frost-hardy varieties
	April	tender varieties
Leeks	Jan–Feb	early varieties
	Feb–Mar	late varieties
Lettuce	Jan–July	
Marrows	April	
Onions	Feb–Mar	
Peas	Feb–June	
Runner beans	April	
Savoy cabbage	April–May	
Sweet corn	April	
Tomatoes – outdoor	Mar	

HARDY VEGETABLES

Hardy vegetables, such as lettuce, cabbage, cauliflower, brussels sprouts, leeks and onions, all of which have small seeds, can be sown in the same way as hardy bedding plants – in pots, with the seedlings being pricked out into trays later.

Although they will germinate without any heat, the seeds do come up better if they are kept in a frost-free greenhouse, or a heated propagator. This is especially useful if you are making very early sowings.

A temperature of 16°C (60°F) is all that is needed; in fact lettuce may not germinate at higher temperatures than this. Large seeded hardy vegetables, such as peas and beans, are best space sown – that is the seeds should be spaced out about 2·5–5 cm (1–2 in) apart in rows in a seed tray. This way there is no need to prick out the seedlings. The young plants should be planted out in the garden as soon as you see roots beginning to grow through the holes in the bottom of their tray.

French beans and other half-hardy vegetables will not survive a frost or cold weather, so raise seedlings in the greenhouse and plant outside in milder weather. 'Blue Lake' French beans, shown here, are ready for picking.

Globe artichokes have a better chance of surviving if you grow from seed in a greenhouse instead of sowing directly in the garden. When seedlings are large enough to handle, prick them out into pots. Transplant to the garden when danger of frost has passed.

To space sow, fill the tray with seed compost, space the seeds out over the surface, and press them lightly into the surface so that they are just covered with compost. Water them in, and treat as usual from then on. These seeds, too, germinate without extra heat, but if it is available, they will come up much faster and better. Again, the young plants need to be planted as soon as the tray is filled with roots. There is no need to wait until after the risk of frost, though as usual it pays to plant during a good spell of weather.

HALF-HARDY VEGETABLES

If you want to grow half-hardy vegetables, such as marrows, sweet corn or French beans, a frost-free greenhouse is necessary, and a heated propagator will come in very useful.

Because the plants will not withstand any frost, it is essential to sow at precisely the right time so that the plants are ready to be set out as soon as the weather is warm enough for them. They are generally quite fast growing plants – if

For top quality Savoy cabbages, raise the seedlings in a frost-free greenhouse or, even better, an electric propagator. Sow the seed in spring and plant out in summer for harvesting during the winter.

'Vegetable Spaghetti', a variety of squash, will thrive if grown under glass. To eat this intriguing vegetable you boil it whole for 25 minutes, then cut it in half and fork out the spaghetti-like strands.

you live in the south of the country and want plants to put out in mid May, sow from early to mid April. Further north, you should sow up to two weeks later.

As half-hardy vegetables mainly have large seeds, they can be space sown in trays, in the same way as peas and beans. But for even better results, sow two or three seeds in a 9 cm (3½ in) pot, and remove all but the strongest seedlings when they come up. This way, if the weather is too cold when the pots are filled with root, you can move them into larger pots, and continue growing them under glass for another week or two if need be, without them coming to harm.

TREES AND SHRUBS
Raising your own trees and shrubs from scratch is a rewarding pastime, as well as

an inexpensive way of stocking a garden or producing plants for a new hedge. Although young plants could be propagated outside in the vegetable garden or in a cold frame, they will grow much faster under glass.

They are also safer under glass, where there is less risk of them being overwhelmed by weeds, or destroyed by mice, rabbits or slips of the hoe. A cold greenhouse is all you need, plus a good deal of patience. Although some of the faster growing shrubs may be ready for planting after a year, many kinds take longer.

TREES AND SHRUBS FROM SEED
A huge range of trees and shrubs can now be grown from seed, which is readily available to the amateur gardener. The majority of seed firms despatch seeds

Bush tomato plants grow without extra support, but it can be difficult to see the crop among the thick foliage.

during the spring months, and this is the most suitable time to sow them.

Germination Sow them in pots in exactly the same way as usual, but cover the seeds with a thin layer of horticultural sand. Water in, and keep the pots moist, and in a shady spot. Some may germinate within a few weeks, but don't worry if they take longer – many trees and shrubs are notoriously slow to come through.

Many kinds won't germinate at all until after a prolonged cold spell. This is nature's way of ensuring that the young seedlings only come up in spring, and not just before the start of bad weather. There

'Tennessee Waltz',
like other fuchsia
hybrids, can be
increased by taking
cuttings of young

shoots any time
between spring and
early autumn. Use
only the best plants.

are two ways of tackling this delay. One is
to be patient, and put the pots of seeds
outside in the garden (keeping them
watered in the meantime) until the following spring. Then if you bring them in
around February or March, and put them
into the heated propagator at 16°–21°C
(60°–70°F) they should come up within a
few weeks. In an unheated or frost-free
greenhouse they'll take a bit longer.

The other alternative is to fool the seeds
into thinking that winter has come and
gone, by popping them into the fridge for

four to six weeks. To work properly, the
seed must be either sown in a pot or mixed
with some sand, and kept moist during
this treatment. Just putting the packet of
seed into the fridge does not work. (To
prevent domestic objections, you can
always put the pots of seed inside polythene bags.)

When the seeds do come up, there is no
need to prick them out straight away
provided they are well spaced out. They
normally do better left to grow on for a
while without being disturbed.

Potting up and potting on The best
time to pot seedlings is in the autumn, just
after they stop growing, or early the
following spring. Use 9 cm (3½ in) pots and
John Innes potting compost No. 2, and

grow them on in slight shade, keeping the
young plants just moist all the time.

When the original containers are full of
root, pot them on to 13 cm (5 in) pots. If
you have a lot of plants and don't want
to go to the expense of buying plastic
pots, use the type that look like black
polythene bags – these are sold in garden
centres very cheaply.

Cultivation Feed and water the young
plants well during the growing season,
from spring to late autumn, but keep them
almost dry in winter. If space permits,
grow the young plants on in a well-shaded
and well ventilated greenhouse in summer, and in winter – this will make them
grow fast. But if you need the room,
plunge rows of pots up to their rims in
the soil in the vegetable garden. And
don't forget they still need regular feeding
and watering.

Different species will grow at different
rates, but the first should be ready to plant
out 18–24 months after sowing. It is fairly
important not to plant young trees and
shrubs out until they are about the same
size as those you would buy from a garden
centre. In your home 'nursery' young
plants will automatically get regular attention, but out in the garden they are
more likely to be left to fend for themselves, and unless they are reasonably big
there is a high risk of losing them if you
plant them out too soon.

**TREES AND SHRUBS FROM
CUTTINGS**
Although seeds are a cheap way of adding
new trees and shrubs to the garden, cuttings will give you much faster results. In
some cases you will have plants that are
ready to put out within a year, provided
you choose fast growing kinds. The draw-
back, however, is that you will need to
find a suitable source of cuttings in
the first place.

Availability You can use plants in
your own garden, or those belonging to
friends. Alternatively, join a horticultural
society and arrange to make swaps with
other members. You can sometimes buy
tree and shrub cuttings that are already
rooted. These just need potting and growing on, following the same method given
below after rooting your own cuttings.

Suitable varieties Not all shrubs are easy to root from cuttings. As a rough guide, you can reckon plants that are expensive to buy are difficult to propagate. Trees and shrubs that grow particularly quickly and easily from cuttings include lavender, shrubby sages (*Salvia*), hardy fuchsias, rosemary, hydrangea, hebe, rue (*Ruta*) and cistus. Moderately easy, though a bit slower to root, are dogwood (*Cornus*), butterfly bush (*Buddleia*), Mexican orange blossom (*Choisya ternata*), smokebush (*Cotinus coggygria*), hypericum, mahonia, shrubby potentillas, flowering currants (*Ribes*), alder (*Sambucus*), escallonia, rose species, berberis, pyracantha, forsythia, weigela, willows (*Salix*) and poplars. (Always take more cuttings than you need, to allow for the inevitable losses.)

There are two seasons when shrub cuttings root particularly well – mid summer and early autumn. The techniques used are the same for both groups, but the first root and grow quicker, so they are best kept separate from the others for ease of working.

MID SUMMER CUTTINGS
In June and July the new growth is still soft, so take softwood cuttings in the same way as you would of a geranium or fuchsia. Use secateurs to cut 10 cm (4 in) lengths from the tips of strong, healthy looking shoots. Put them straight into a

New growth and a healthy appearance indicate that fuchsia cuttings have rooted. Pot them on into individual pots immediately – a long delay may check their growth. Where cuttings have been taken from several varieties, make sure you label them.

polythene bag to stop them wilting while you finish collecting your other cuttings.

Back at the greenhouse, prepare the cuttings using a very sharp knife to cut cleanly just beneath a leaf joint, and remove the leaves from the lower half of the stem. Dip the base of each cutting in hormone rooting powder, and push four to six of them around the edge of a 13 cm (5 in) pot filled with a mix of 50 per cent sharp horticultural sand and 50 per cent sedge peat. Water them in, and spray the foliage with fungicide solution immediately afterwards. From then on, keep the cuttings humid, shaded, and well ventilated so they don't get too hot.

General care A good place to root shrub cuttings in summer is under the staging, provided the greenhouse has glass down to ground level. They should

HARDWOOD CUTTINGS

1. Take 15–20 cm (6–8 in) hardwood cuttings from shrubs in September. Trim the base of the shoot below a leaf joint.

2. Pinch out the soft growing tip, using your thumb and finger, and then remove most of the lower leaves.

3. Push the cuttings into a prepared bed in the greenhouse border, leaving 2·5–5 cm (1–2 in) showing above ground.

be kept constantly just moist. Check daily to see if watering is needed, but avoid over-watering or they may rot. To prevent the leaves from wilting, keep the air around the cuttings humid by spraying them with water every morning, or by damping down the floor of the greenhouse. An effective way of keeping shrub cuttings both moist and humid is by standing the pots on damp capillary matting. Also spray the cuttings fortnightly with fungicide as a precaution to stop grey mould and other fungal diseases developing. If any are seen remove affected leaves or cuttings at once.

The easier cuttings should be fairly well rooted in about six weeks; others may take a few weeks longer. You can easily tell when cuttings have rooted, as suddenly the leaves look plump and healthy, and the young plants start to grow. You will also see roots beginning to grow out through the hole in the base of the pot.

Growing on When the cuttings are well rooted, pot each one individually into a 9 cm ($3\frac{1}{2}$ in) pot filled with potting compost. Don't leave them too long in the original pot as the peat/sand mixture in which they were rooted does not contain any plant foods.

Increase your stock of herbs by taking semi-ripe cuttings from shrubby species – bay, sage, rosemary and rue – in summer. Pot in a peat and sand mix.

The staging of a well-ventilated and well-shaded greenhouse makes a good site for growing on shrub cuttings. In summer feed and water them well, but during the winter keep them almost dry.

Grow the young plants on in the same way as suggested for shrubs raised from seed (see page 81). Feed and water them well, and pot on to 13 cm (5 in) pots when they need it. Stop the new shoots once or twice to make the plants become bushy. Plant them out when they are as big as the ones you might buy commercially.

EARLY AUTUMN CUTTINGS

By September, the parent plants you take your cuttings from will not be growing as fast as in summer. The shoots will be woodier, deciduous plants will be about to shed their leaves, and there will not be enough time for cuttings to get well rooted before the winter rest starts. So it pays to make a few small modifications to the method, since these are hardwood shrub cuttings.

Preparation Instead of putting the cuttings into pots, it is far better to place them straight into a prepared bed in the border. To prepare the bed, fork plenty of peat and horticultural grit into the soil. This will turn it into a good rooting compost.

If the greenhouse can conveniently be emptied, now is a good time to give it a thorough cleaning. Drench the cuttings' bed with a garden disinfectant, such as Jeyes Fluid, to get rid of any diseased organisms. Leave it for a few days, then fork the soil over and wait until the smell of the disinfectant has completely cleared before taking cuttings.

Method Make the cuttings a little longer than before, about 15–45 cm (6–8 in) long. Use a sharp knife to cut the base of the cuttings neatly just below a leaf joint. Then pinch out the growing tip of each shoot, so you remove all the soft, half-grown leaves and only full size leaves remain. Next, remove the leaves from all but the top layer of each cutting.

Dip the base of the cuttings in rooting powder, and push them into the prepared bed, to within 2·5 cm (1 in) of their tops, in a row, spaced about 15 cm (6 in) apart. Water them in, and spray the tops with fungicide as before. Water only lightly in winter, just enough to stop them drying out completely. Don't disturb them until spring, when cuttings that start growing strongly can be dug up carefully and potted. Grow them on as for summer cuttings, leaving unrooted cuttings longer.

85

PESTS AND DISEASES UNDER GLASS

When you put up a new greenhouse, you are unlikely to be troubled much by pests or diseases, as it takes time for the house to be colonized by them. But after a year or so, the odd problem will undoubtedly crop up. If you know what to expect, and are properly equipped to tackle these as soon as they arise, you will always be able to keep plants healthy – without using any more chemicals than necessary. One point to bear in mind is that not all greenhouse problems are caused by pests and diseases alone. Some are growing problems, that are best prevented by correct cultivation.

PESTS

The majority of common greenhouse insect pests can be tackled effectively by spraying with any good systemic insecticide, but don't be afraid to take advice on individual brands from a professional. Some insect pests, such as whitefly and red spider mite, are persistent and need spraying at regular intervals.

Natural control Insects can also be controlled without chemicals, by encouraging natural insect predators, such as ladybirds, lacewings and hoverflies, to do the job for you. If you want to use natural pest control, the best plan is to stop using chemicals anywhere in the garden, and plant lots of brightly coloured flowers that provide a good nectar feed for the adult insects – French marigolds (*Tagetes*) are particularly good for encouraging beneficial insects.

Many of these beneficial insects will then find their way inside the greenhouse whenever the ventilators or door are open, but to encourage them in, try planting a few French marigolds in the greenhouse

A clump of French marigolds in a greenhouse will attract nectar-feeding insects whose larvae are predators of greenfly.

border too. Other useful natural predators to encourage are centipedes and black beetles – they remove many harmful insects at ground level.

Outside in the garden, encourage frogs, toads, hedgehogs and garden birds to visit. They will consume vast quantities of slugs and snails, cutting down the chances of these pests attacking plants in the greenhouse. Bluetits will clean large numbers of greenfly from roses and fruit trees, again making it less likely the insects will find their way into the greenhouse.

The biggest problem with natural pest control is that it takes a while for the numbers of beneficial insects to build up to a useful level. If you do have a serious outbreak of greenfly to contend with in the meantime, you may have to spray in order to save plants from being ruined. In this case, use a product based on pirimicarb that is harmless to beneficial insects.

COMMON GREENHOUSE PESTS

Ants They can be a nuisance if they take up residence in a pot, when they remove much of the compost in the process of building a nest. Use ant powder, or if the nest is accessible try pouring boiling water into it.

Birds They can be a problem in summer when the greenhouse door and ventilators are open. They may peck ripening tomatoes or grapes, or uproot seedlings. Deter them by fixing netting over vents and door or by hanging a curtain of plastic strips over the doorway.

Caterpillars Rarely much of a problem under glass, though they can occasionally make holes in leaves or tomatoes. Culprits can often be found and removed by hand, without spraying.

Greenfly Tiny green, pink or brown insects which do not fly, and are found on the growing tips of shoots or under young leaves. Most plants are affected, especially those with soft leaves. Any systemic insecticide will control them, or use a product based on pirimicarb where you want to protect beneficial insects.

Mice More of a problem in winter and early spring, especially in country districts. Mice will remove any seeds large enough to eat, but especially peas and beans, which are often buried in the border for later germination. They will also eat small seedlings. Use poisonous bait, traditional traps, or the new humane mouse traps which catch mice, letting you later release them unharmed.

Mushroom fly Small black flies that gather in clouds round potted plants. The adults are harmless but lay their eggs in pots, particularly in peat-based composts. The larvae feed on young roots and can do much damage to small seedlings. Protect plants by watering the compost with a solution of malathion, made up to the same strength as you would use for spraying. This should also kill the larvae while they are small.

An infestation of whitefly has caused the edges of these geranium leaves to turn yellow. The plants will eventually be weakened but, except in severe cases, not killed.

Left: Scale insects, which attach themselves to the undersides of leaves, can be removed with a cloth.

Above: The mottling on the leaves of this busy Lizzy is the result of red spider mites.

Red spider mite   Minute non-flying insects, almost invisible to the naked eye, cause leaves to turn yellow and drop off. In severe cases, small fine webs can be seen at the tips of shoots. They are particularly common on cucumbers, fuchsias and ivies, though most plants can be affected. Spray with a product containing pirimiphos-methyl.

Scale insect   Less common in a mixed collection, this limpet-like insect about 3 mm ($\frac{1}{8}$ in) long attaches itself to stems and leaves of waxy leaved plants such as citrus. Spray with systemic insecticide.

Slugs and snails   Among the worst pests under glass. They will make holes in the leaves of mature plants, and often eat

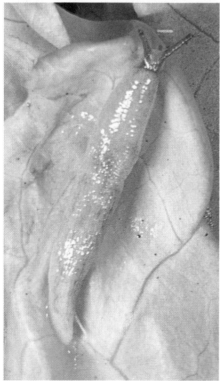

Left: If you see slugs on lettuce leaves, pick them off before they cause any damage.

Above: A colony of greenfly on a house plant can be sprayed with a systemic insecticide.

small seedlings entirely. To prevent slug damage, sprinkle slug pellets very thinly under staging and in the border between plants, or use one of the new products based on aluminium sulphate which are kinder to wildlife. You can also put out an old-fashioned slug trap: a saucer of beer in which slugs and snails will drown.

Vine weevil Adults are rarely seen. The larvae, however, are fat white C-shaped grubs often found in pots, especially of cyclamen and primula, though other plants may be affected too. They feed on roots; affected plants turn yellow and wilt rapidly. Protect vulnerable species by watering on a solution of a product containing heptenophos and permethrin in spring.

Whitefly Small white, moth-like flying insects found underneath young leaves, especially on fuchsias, though many other plants are affected too. Spray frequently with a product containing permethrin or pirimiphos-methyl.

Woodlice Small creatures, 6–13 mm ($\frac{1}{4}$–$\frac{1}{2}$ in) long, that roll up into balls when disturbed. It is said they do not harm plants, only feeding on decaying vegetation. However, it is best to play safe by clearing away rubbish where they can hide, and keeping the greenhouse as clean and tidy as possible to discourage them from taking up residence.

DISEASES

Plant diseases are most common in early spring, autumn and winter, when the air is cold and damp and light levels are low. You can prevent many diseases by keeping the greenhouse clean and tidy, and removing dead leaves and flowers from

89

plants as soon as they are seen. It is also a good idea to keep the greenhouse well ventilated, and to avoid watering plants except when absolutely necessary in winter. Much damping off in seedlings can be avoided by sowing later in spring rather than trying to make too early a start.

COMMON PLANT DISEASES

Damping off (seedlings) This is commonest in early spring. Ensure seed trays, pots and propagators are kept scrupulously clean, and rinse before use with garden disinfectant such as Jeyes Fluid. Ventilate the propagators as soon as seedlings start germinating. Avoid keeping early sown seedlings too wet. If damping off starts, spray with copper fungicide or cheshunt compound.

Grey mould Light grey fluff found growing on leaves, fruit or flowers at any time of the year, but particularly when humidity is high and light levels are low. Spray with systemic fungicide such as benomyl or thiophanate-methyl.

Neck rot Commonest on young melons and cucumbers, and plants with soft fleshy stems such as cacti and succulents. It is often caused by keeping plants too wet when they are young, in winter when they are resting, or whenever growing conditions are not good. Avoid neck rot by not overwatering at these times. Plants such as cacti can often be treated by cutting away the top of the plant, and re-rooting it. With other kinds of plants cuttings can sometimes be taken to save them.

Powdery mildew is a white powder-like mould which appears on leaves when the weather is dull. It is very common in the autumn months.

Powdery mildew Talcum-like powder on upper surfaces of leaves, especially cucumbers, though other plants can be affected too. It is mainly a problem in autumn. Spray with benomyl, thiophanate-methyl, carbendazin or liquid copper.

Root rot Again, this may be caused by overwatering. The fine root hairs that take water into the plant are killed, so the plant wilts although it has plenty of water. Affected plants may recover if you allow the compost to dry out and keep it drier than usual for a few weeks while new root hairs grow.

Root rot can also be caused by organisms in the soil if the same crops, such as tomatoes, are repeatedly grown in the same site. Avoid this problem by growing crops in a different place each year, by replacing the top 45 cm (18 in) of border soil every year, or by using growing bags for a few years.

OTHER COMMON PROBLEMS

Moss or algae When growing on the compost it normally indicates overwatering – remove it by hand, and keep affected plants slightly drier in future. Make sure watering cans are not left full of water, as algae which develops inside can then spread into plant pots every time you water. Prevent it from forming by washing out the can periodically with garden disinfectant and rinse before use.

Algae and moss growing on the glass or structure of the greenhouse may indicate prolonged high humidity, but it is more usually a sign that the greenhouse is ready for its annual spring clean. Remove plants and scrub down the inside of the house (the glass panes and the frame) and staging with warm water and garden disinfectant, rinse well with clean water, and return the plants.

Over/underwatering In both cases plants are likely to show similar symptoms – poor growth and yellowing leaves which eventually drop off. Check the plants daily to see if they need watering, instead of guessing, and aim to keep the pots evenly moist in summer, and dryish in winter. Remember that overwatering, is a common cause of plant failure.

If incorrect watering is a frequent problem, it is a good idea to invest in a water meter to help you get it right, or to change the kind of compost you use. Note that soil-based composts, such as John Innes, dry out fast and need plenty of water, whereas the peat-based kinds hold water for longer and therefore should be watered more sparingly.

Sun scorch This can be fatal to young plants and seedlings, and causes unsightly beige marks on leaves of older plants where areas of tissue have been killed. To prevent scorch, always keep young seedlings and cuttings shaded from direct sun, and shade newly potted plants for a week or two until they are well established. Some plants, such as streptocarpus and ferns, need to be grown in slightly shaded

Plant diseases, like the fungal infection on this ivy, can be prevented by removing all dead leaves as soon as you see them.

conditions throughout their lives.

Plants most at risk can be protected from scorch by growing them under the staging in summer (they will get enough light if in an all-glass greenhouse), by shading the glass with a liquid shading paint, or by shading part of the house with an old net curtain or sheet.

Badly scorched plants usually die, but those only slightly affected can often be treated by cutting off the most badly damaged leaves. Then put the plant in a

cool, shady place, and water well until it starts growing again.

TOMATO PROBLEMS

Unlike most greenhouse plants that are reasonably trouble free much of the time, tomatoes have a large collection of problems you can expect to come across sooner or later.

Flowers that open but do not set fruit may not have been properly pollinated.

Paint liquid shading over part of the greenhouse in summer to prevent the sun scorching young plants.

This is a common problem with early planted crops in heated greenhouses. You must spray the flowers with water from a hosepipe on fine days or use a hormone fruit setting spray.

Flowers that drop off without opening may be affected by grey mould – spray with benomyl.

Above: Erratic watering of tomato plants can cause fruits to split or crack when they ripen.

Right: Spray plants in the early morning or late afternoon when the sun is not too strong.

SPRAYING HINTS AND TIPS

If you have to spray, always follow the manufacturer's instructions on dilution rate and how often to apply the product. As a general rule, whenever you spray:

● Avoid spraying in bright sunlight/ when plants have been kept very dry, or they may scorch – early morning or late evening is the best time to spray.

● Always make sure you spray in good time; don't wait until damage is severe or it will take plants longer to recover, and they will be left with marked leaves which are unlikely to improve.

● Check the instructions on the bottle to ensure that the spray you are using is suitable for the plants you want to treat. If any plants are known to be sensitive to a particular product, these will be listed in the manufacturer's instructions.

● Always keep a separate sprayer for weedkillers – however well you wash the sprayer out afterwards, there is a risk that a trace may remain that will damage or kill greenhouse plants.

Tomato plants that grow lots of leaf but no flowers may have been planted too soon. Next time delay planting until the first truss (bunch) of flowers has opened.

Small pale coloured spots on ripe or unripe fruit is ghost spot, caused by grey mould. Affected fruit are perfectly all right to eat. You cannot treat spotted fruit, but prevent it by spraying with benomyl, particularly in warm, humid weather.

Split or cracked fruit are caused by uneven watering, where plants alternate between being too wet and too dry. The results do not show until some time later, so it is difficult to find out when it may have happened. Avoid the problem by keeping plants uniformly moist – if necessary use an automatic watering system.

Blotchy green patches on otherwise ripe fruit is blotchy ripening – this can be caused by insufficient potash, in which case increase the amount of feed you are giving and be sure to use a special high potash liquid tomato feed. It can also be caused by premature ripening if the plants have had their lower leaves removed – do not take off any leaves unless they have turned yellow.

INDEX

ACKNOWLEDGEMENTS

The Publishers wish to thank the following for providing photographs in this book:
Baco Ltd/Tony Brabner 13; Eric Crichton 11t, 17, 31, 33b, 36, 38b, 54b, 55, 56, 57, 58, 61, 63tl&b, 65, 66, 67, 68t, 88, 89t, 93t; The Garden Picture Library/R Sutherland 6; Photos Horticultural 20, 27, 62, 71, 79t, 80b, 89b, 90; The Harry Smith Collection 46, 48; Peter Stiles 28, 29t, 38t, 54t, 63tr, 81; Suttons Seeds Ltd 50, 51r.

The following photographs were taken specially for the Octopus Publishing Group Picture Library:
7, 25, 51l, 91; M Boys 10, 15b, 32t, 41, 44, 49, 72, 74, 76, 78, 79b, 84, 85; M Crockett 15t, 16, 23, 26, 93b; J Harpur 11b, 37, 59b, 92; Neil Holmes 8, 12, 18, 21, 30, 34, 35, 39, 40, 42, 43, 47, 53, 60, 68b, 73t, 80t, 83, 86; John Moss 52; John Sims 87; George Wright 32b, 33t, 59t, 64, 73b, 75, 77, 82.